PURPOSE BY DESIGN

USING HUMAN DESIGN TO DISCOVER YOUR TRUE NATURE

HUMAN DESIGN THOUGHT LEADERS
with Karen Curry Parker

Edited by Laurie Knight
Cover design by Kristina Edstrom

An Imprint for GracePoint Publishing (www.GracePointPublishing.com)

GracePoint Matrix, LLC
624 S. Cascade Ave. Suite 201, Colorado Springs, CO 80903
www.GracePointMatrix.com
Email: Admin@GracePointMatrix.com
SAN # 991-6032

A Library of Congress Control Number has been requested and is pending.

ISBN: (Paperback) 978-1-955272-78-0
eISBN: 978-1-955272-77-3

Books may be purchased for educational, business, or sales promotional use.
For bulk order requests and price schedule contact:
Orders@GracePointPublishing.com

Table of Contents

Publisher's Note

When GracePoint Publishing released *Abundance by Design*, the first book in this series in 2016, we knew it would have an impact but did not realize how much. To date, it is still one of our bestselling titles. Human Design is a pathway to understanding the self and sharing stories is a powerful way to encourage someone to take that journey.

As we prepared for the 2022 Human Design Conference and the world was shifting out of COVID lockdown, we knew it was time to publish the next book. When the invitation was sent out to participate in *Purpose by Design*, we attracted thought leaders to whom Human Design was a significant part of their journey.

If this book has found you and you are not familiar with Human Design, these authors have numerous resources to help you understand the basics. A great place to start is by getting your chart at freehumandesignchart.com. Then, at the end of every chapter, each author has provided their contact information and more about how they can support you on your journey.

Being aligned with your purpose is a key part of healing and growth, and we hope this book supports you in that journey.

What a pleasure to publish this amazing resource!

Tascha Yoder

Director of Publishing, GracePoint Publishing

Introduction

By Karen Curry Parker

My great-grandmother was a midwife in Appalachia. She rode through the Blue Ridge Mountains on horseback taking care of young mothers. When a woman came near her "time," my great-grandmother would pack up her saddlebags, ride over the hills, and live with the expectant family, cooking and cleaning while waiting for the arrival of the baby.

Between midwifery gigs, my great-grandmother was also a revival preacher. While she waited for babies to be born, she would enlist the local community to pitch a tent and, on Sundays, she would climb a small wooden box so that her four-foot, ten-inch body could be seen above the crowd while she preached the gospel.

I followed in my great-grandmother's footsteps and started my career as a midwife until I fell in love with Human Design. While I never became a revival preacher, I approached teaching Human Design with the same zest and zealousness as my great-grandmother preaching and saving lost souls.

In the beginning of my Human Design career, I preached that everyone has a purpose and that finding your purpose is the only thing you need to unlock passion, action, and direction in your life. I truly believed that if you just "lived" your purpose you would do amazing things, never procrastinate again, make wild profits, and have ample energy to fulfill every desire and intention that crossed your mind. I embraced terms like being *purpose-driven* and, in my oh-so-Manifesting-Generator-way, taught that purpose was something that a person had to "do."

No matter how hard I preached purpose and profit, purpose and action, purpose and work, and living a purpose-driven life, my clients still didn't "do" their purpose. This frustrated me and caused me to preach louder from my "purpose pulpit."

At the time when I was preaching purpose, most of my clients were Projectors. It didn't take long for the Projectors to put me in my place. They clearly let me know that they couldn't *do* their purpose. It didn't feel right. They didn't have the energy and no amount of *knowing* their purpose could help them put it into some kind of profitable, purpose-driven action.

I had no choice but to return to the Human Design chart to figure out what was actually going on. Why was "doing" your purpose so hard?

Human Design teaches that your life and soul purpose are encoded in two crystalline bodies of energy called the Design Crystal and the Personality Crystal. These aren't actual physical crystals but codes of information that help define who you are in this lifetime.

At the moment of your conception, your father's energy calls forth a crystalline code of energy that resides in the Earth. This crystalline code of energy, called the Design Crystal, contains the code for your human life story and purpose. It initiates and manages the process of the development of your body as you grow from undifferentiated cells into a baby. The Design Crystal carries your gene codes, your epigenetic programming, your ancestral memories, and all the things that make your unique human story.

The Design Crystal is bundled with a special magnet called the Magnetic Monopole. The Magnetic Monopole is a magnetic force that only attracts. Your Magnetic Monopole is encoded with the information that will attract into your life all the experiences you are destined to have that are essential to your life story. The Magnetic Monopole is also the source of the Law of Attraction.

The events in life that have seemed fated or part of an unavoidable destiny are encoded in the Magnetic Monopole. As we evolve, our ability to consciously program our Monopole is growing, and we are gaining more control over what we attract into our lives.

The third component, the Personality Crystal, contains the code for your soul purpose. It enters the body at the moment of your birth.

At birth, the Design Crystal takes up residence in the Ajna Center. The Magnetic Monopole resides in the G Center, and the Personality Crystal is in the Head Center.

The combination of the Design Crystal, the Personality Crystal, and the Magnetic Monopole help define the field of choices over the course of your life. The full range of potentials you can choose for your life is extensive, and you certainly won't run out of options in what you create in your reality! This limitation of possibilities is significant because it helps define who you perceive yourself to be in your current incarnation.

This combination of codes also makes you a unique once-in-a-lifetime cosmic event!

Just like we all carry the entire human genome, we all have all of the Human Design chart. Openness (the white parts of the chart) is simply energy that we experience from others. Definition (the colored parts of the chart) is part of our life curriculum and what we learn about from our own life experiences. The chart itself is a blueprint for the potential of the entire human story. In this next section we are going to explore the chart as a blueprint. What I'm going to share with you about purpose in the chart is true of all of us and isn't dependent on what is defined or open in your personal chart.

To live your life as the fullest expression of the potential of your Human Design chart *is your purpose*, but there are two centers in the chart that give you a lot of information about what you *need* to truly fulfill your purpose.

The two centers associated with purpose are the Will Center and the G Center. Both of these two centers correlate with the heart chakra in the Hindu chakra system. Our purpose.

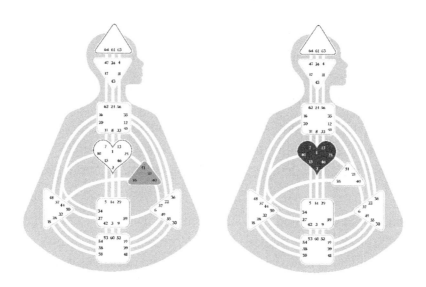

The Will Center, associated with our physical heart, represents our personal identity and our unique life purpose. The G Center, associated with what is often referred to as the "high heart" by energy medicine practitioners, represents our Higher Self or our soul's purpose.

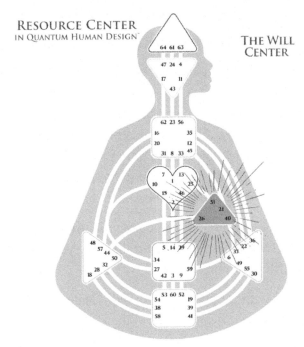

RESOURCE CENTER
IN QUANTUM HUMAN DESIGN™

THE WILL
CENTER

The Will Center corresponds with the ego. The ego is often associated with its shadow expressions of swagger, selfishness, and narcissism. In truth, the Will Center is the center tied to our sense of value, self-worth, and sustainability. This shadow expression of ego is a symptom of overcompensating for low self-worth.

The ego, represented by the Will Center is essential for fulfilling your purpose. Your personal self is essential to fulfilling the bigger role that you play in the Cosmic Plan. Your ego represents your personal identity, the you who is here to implement your part of the Cosmic Plan.

The Will Center is also associated with sustainability. The Will Center gives us energy in cycles. The healthy use of will invites us to explore the balance between work and rest. When we have a healthy sense of self-worth, we value ourselves enough to take care of ourselves, rest, and play. We inherently understand that to fulfill our unique and vital role in the world, we must rest and nurture ourselves in order to be sustainable.

The Will Center is where we experience the physical manifestation of turning value into form. This is the center that regulates the energy of money, possessions, resources, and commerce. It is a very material energy center that lends itself to measuring value with things and numbers. In the shadow of this energy, we take our value from how much money we have or how many possessions we own.

One way to understand these energies and how they work together is through the concept of endurance. To keep generating resources and material goods, we need to have sustainable energy. To have sustainable energy, we must rest. To rest, we must believe that our contribution to the world is so valuable that we are worthy of resting enough to sustain it. Any disruption in this cycle, and we find ourselves pushing with energy we don't have and potentially burning out.

Not only that, if we spend our energy trying to prove our value or hiding our authentic self because we don't believe in our value, we run the risk of using our vital energy to maintain a facade. Anytime you say yes when you want to say no, anytime you pretend to be someone or something you're not, and anytime you devalue who you were born to be, you use your energy to hide out instead of expressing yourself and you run the risk of burning out.

Interestingly, there is also mysticism in this center, which helps us to better understand the ego. By nature, we each have a differentiated ego (or human self), and this differentiation says, "I'm part of the puzzle, and I have to do my part very well to be of service to the greater good." And so, we are meant to surrender our ego and use our uniqueness as a foundation for service toward the well-being of others. This may look like supporting people financially and materially, as well as through other resources like teaching or providing clean water and air. When we surrender the energies of the Will Center (such as money, things of value, the ego, personal willpower, etc.) to something greater than ourselves, we allow our individual lives to serve the betterment of others.

Contemplations for the Will Center:

- Do you value yourself?
- Do you trust Source?
- How do you measure your value?
- What needs to be healed, released, aligned, or brought to your awareness for you to know your unique, vital, and irreplaceable role in the Cosmic Plan?

The G Center, associated with the liver and blood, represents our higher purpose and the themes that highlight the potential of our collective human story. The shadow of the G Center can cause you to question your lovability and challenge your self-acceptance. The shadow of the G Center can also make you feel lost or directionless.

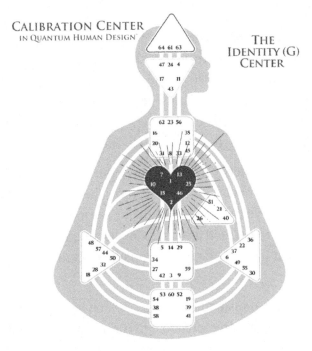

The G Center is the center for love and direction. We literally take our direction from love. The G Center shows us that personal narrative is essential to living aligned with our purpose. In other words, the stories we tell about who we are (our identity), set the tone and the direction for what we attract into our lives.

The G Center is the seat of the Magnetic Monopole, the magnetic force that attracts experiences into your life. Love is the force that calibrates the Monopole, influencing the kinds of experiences and relationships you call into your life. The more you love yourself and others and take back control over the story you tell about who you are, the more you calibrate your Heart to attract what you need to fulfill your story.

One of the most interesting things to note about the G Center is that it isn't a motorized center. It has no energy for *doing*, only *being*. When we "be" who we decide we want to be and we love and value ourselves, we calibrate the magnetic resonance field of the Heart (Magnetic Monopole) to bring us experiences that match our personal narrative.

There is nothing we have to "do" except make sure that we craft a darn good story about who we are, a story that includes a high degree of self-love and self-worth. The more we love ourselves and value ourselves, the more we calibrate our Heart to create a life that reflects our lovability and our value.

Contemplations for the G Center:

- Do you feel accepted for who you are?
- Do you compromise who you are to please others?
- Do you feel safe to be yourself fully?
- Do you feel lovable?
- What stories do you tell about who you are? Are they good stories? Are they stories that are true and worthy of you? Do you need to rewrite any of them to make them better?

Purpose also lives in two channels in the Human Design chart. The first channel is the 25/51, the Channel of Initiation in traditional Human Design, and the Channel of Higher Purpose in Quantum Human Design™. The second channel is the 1/8, the Channel of Inspiration in Traditional Human Design, and the Channel of Self-Fulfillment in Quantum Human Design™.

51/25–Channel of Initiation | Channel of Higher Purpose

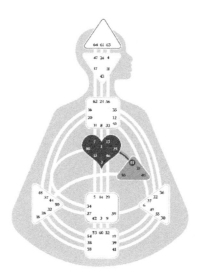

This powerful channel connecting the Will Center to the G Center is often referred to as the Channel of the Shaman or Priest/Priestess. In the metaphor of the shaman, the shaman "dies" to the personal self (ego) and emerges aligned with their higher purpose.

This channel shows us that to fulfill your higher purpose you must transcend your personal experiences and life's disruptions and to see them as catalysts that help you align with your higher purpose. The process of discovering the value of your life and allowing the ego to serve the Higher Self helps you use your life to serve the heart's direction and purpose; to align life with love.

The journey illuminated by this channel reminds us that we are here to serve something bigger than our personal life story, but, at the same time, it reminds us that our personal life story is an essential part of something bigger.

Maturity, wisdom, and the fulfillment of purpose happen when you discover that your life is essential to the well-being of the world. When you stop trying to prove your value and learn to trust that you are here as a once-in-a-lifetime cosmic event, you start contributing the beauty and the value of who you are to the beauty of the world.

Contemplations for the 51/25:

- Do you trust Source?
- Can you find the higher purpose in your life experiences?
- How have your past experiences helped you contribute to others?
- How have your past experiences initiated you into a deeper understanding of your purpose?

1/8–Channel of Inspiration | Channel of Self-Fulfillment

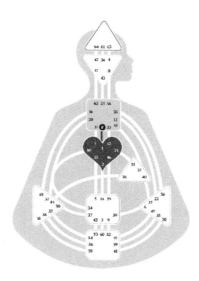

This channel is often associated with creativity. We often associate creativity with arts and crafts, but in truth, we are all creatives, crafting our lives and contributing to the world through the fulfillment of the potential of our personal story and maximizing the relentlessly authentic expression of who we were born to be.

There is tremendous fear and pressure in this channel. The fear here is that we are "failing" our life purpose and mission. If we are mistakenly pushing to fulfill our life purpose by trying to "do" it, instead of "be" it, we run the risk of feeling anxious and even bitter, struggling to get recognition instead of allowing ourselves to fully embody the story of who we are.

There is also great vulnerability here, especially if you have this channel or any other channel from the G Center to the Throat Center defined (colored in). If you have this in your chart, it means that you speak from your heart. It's a gentle, but powerful configuration that can cause you to hide who you are if you don't feel safe, loved, or accepted for who you are.

The power of this channel lies in the understanding that the contribution you are here to give the world is not anything you *create* or *do*. YOU are the contribution you are here to give the world. Your story, your life experiences, and the authentic embodiment of who you were born to be contributes beauty and well-being to the world. The more relentlessly authentic you are, the more you co-regulate the energy in the spaces you fill, blazing a trail of potential authenticity for everyone around you.

This truly is the purpose of your life—to change and heal the world by being the complete fulfillment of the person you were born to be.

Contemplations for the 1/8:

- Are you honest with the world about who you are?
- What needs to be healed, released, aligned, or brought to your awareness for you to express your Authentic Self more deeply?
- What stories do you have about yourself that need to be rewritten?

Gate 2–The Gate of Allowing

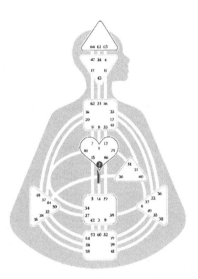

Lastly, I want to give you one important piece of information that might help you defend yourself against any old stories that are keeping you from seeing the necessity for you to fully express who you are in the world.

Gate 2, the gate most closely associated with the Magnetic Monopole, is the most receptive energy in the entire Human Design chart. This gate teaches us that when we are fully and relentlessly authentic in our self-expression, we are designed to receive all the support and resources we need to fulfill the true story of who we were born to be.

The opposite is also true. When we fail to be authentic, hide who we are from the world, and deny the value and the worthiness of our existence, we actually block the flow of abundance and support.

You are literally, designed to be supported in every way when you are true to yourself.

Contemplations for Gate 2:

- Do you believe that you deserve to be supported? If not, what needs to change?
- How much support do you allow into your life?
- Do you ask for help when you need it?
- How much do you trust that you can be fully supported?

It took a while to realize that *purpose by design* isn't about doing, but rather about cultivating the will and the sense of worth to stay true to yourself no matter what happens or what is going on around you.

The chart reveals that purpose lies in becoming the fulfillment of the potential of your unique place in the world. Activating purpose is more about having the courage and the will to have an authentic story about who you are that is bigger and stronger than any limiting beliefs you've been conditioned by.

Not only that, the more you tell the true story of who you are and create your life to be a manifestation of this story, the more you calibrate your heart to expand upon this story. Your purpose is not so much about doing, but preparing, expanding, receiving, and, ultimately, sharing who you are with the world. This process of constantly calibrating and aligning your life with who you are *designed* to be is an expansive and attractive state that has the power to influence the energy in a room without having to say a single word.

Your purpose is elegantly and effortlessly activated when you simply be the person you are designed to be.

This is the pulpit I find myself preaching from these days. Be yourself. Love yourself. Be relentlessly and unapologetically who you were born to be. The simple act of being yourself confers upon you all the support and abundance you need to create the wave of influence you desire. *You being you* matters.

You being you changes the world.

Amen.

Karen Curry Parker

Bestselling Author, TEDx Speaker, Leading
Human Design Teacher, and Community Leader

4/6 Time Bender (Manifesting Generator)

Karen Curry Parker is one of the world's leading Human Design teachers and has authored numerous bestselling Human Design books. She is also an EFT (emotional freedom techniques) practitioner since 2000, life coach since 1998, original student of Ra Uru Hu, a TEDx presenter, the host of the *Quantum rEvolution Podcast* and is the co-founder of GracePoint Publishing.

Karen Curry Parker's core mission is to help people reconnect with their original creativity and teach them how to consciously use language and narrative to increase their vitality and well-being and gain control over their lives. She has a deep love for guiding people to achieve their highest potential and live the life they were designed to live by discovering who they are and activating their authentic life path. Karen leads students to their authentic selves through two certification trainings, the Quantum Human Design™ for Everyone Training System and The Quantum Alignment System™. She also founded the Understanding Human Design Community.

Karen is a mother of eight amazing humans, wife of a genius, and grandmother of two emerging world leaders. She has a BSN in nursing, a BA in journalism, and is currently working on her PhD in integrative health at Quantum University.

Karen encourages readers to continue to expand their knowledge on their own Design but also to keep viewing the world through Quantum Human Design as it can impact and benefit areas of their relationships, work ethic, goal setting, and more.

Expand your awareness by exploring more of her works on Amazon:

bit.ly/KCPBooks

Learn more about how you can join Karen's communities and how Quantum Human Design can help you live your most authentic and rewarding life at:

karencurryparker.teachable.com

Follow Karen on Instagram @KarenCurryParker

Making the Impossible Possible

By Lisa Robinett

I now KNOW that what we think is the impossible can be possible.

Growing up, I always wanted to live in the mountains and on the beach. I was told this wasn't possible—you have to choose one or the other; get your head out of the clouds. I decided not to listen to the naysayers and, luckily, I never internalized any of that. Now I wake up every morning nestled in the Hawaiian mountains. I lie in bed giving my body time to wake up gently. I watch out the window as the sunrise illuminates the dense jungle with brilliant golden light, and wakes up the birds, their happy chirping beckoning me into the day. When I'm ready to get up, I walk downstairs and immediately see a view of only ocean and palm trees out of my living room window.

I wake up happy and excited to get into what the day has in store for me. I live in a home that is my sanctuary, full of high vibrational energy and tons of love. I have fulfilling work that I absolutely love, serving others by empowering them to move into the life of their dreams. I have time to be still. I have time to enjoy my family. I have time to take care of myself and my energy. And, I have time to have fun! I now know my worth, I'm living my purpose, and I show up in the world from a centered and joyful place.

But it wasn't always like this.

When I was young, I had dreams that came true so often that if I dreamed it had snowed, my mother would rush around and put insulation on the pipes to prevent them from freezing, in anticipation of snowfall. I had such vivid childhood dreams that I can remember quite a few of them even better than I can remember a movie I watched last week. I would visit spirits and dragons and otherworldly places, but my favorite dreams by far were always the ones where I was flying. I wasn't in any machine, rather my body flew powered by thoughts—specifically, joyful thoughts and the joyful feelings that those produced. The dreams where I was flying were always the most joy-filled dreams. From a young age, I also had this uncanny knack of just knowing things that I had no logical way of knowing. I could always read people so well, it seemed that I knew them better than they knew themselves, and I was always connecting with animals.

As a child, I had all these psychic and spiritual gifts and abilities,—my claircognizance, empathetic connection and knowing, and animal communication—gifts I didn't know the name for, but possessed. Over time, however, the world reflected back to me that that wasn't "truth" or possible and the gifts faded.

I forgot about them.

In the meantime, as I grew up, I manifested a career as a commercial airline pilot. I'm sure in part because of the joy that was always connected to flying.

Honestly, thinking back, becoming a pilot was actually a leap of faith into intuition, though—I've never thought of it that way until now. It was my last year of college, and one day I was just out in nature and watching the birds and thought how fun it would be if I could fly too! The birds looked so free. I loved how the mere thought made me feel. I loved the feeling stirred up by just thinking of flight. I didn't consciously recall my flying dreams, but I'm sure they are what was driving it.

I looked up flying lessons. I called the one that stood out to me from the directory, and the man who answered was an alumnus from my college, USC. He was so kind, and I scheduled the soonest demo flight available. On the demo flight, we took off from a tiny runway over the dense city of Los Angeles, rose above the fog and the smog, and I could see everything. I felt so alive and so free! I got to fly the plane with the controls for a while under the instructor's guidance, and it was such a rush, so fun! After we landed, I exclaimed, "People would pay me to do this!?" I was hooked and I pursued my airline career doggedly from that moment on.

—————◆—————

As a pilot, I felt like I was very much on purpose. For a long time, it was an extremely joyful career, but after some years, I started to get headaches. They were getting more and more severe when I flew. I would also get pain all over my body. I remember once having such sharp and severe abdominal pain while flying the 737 that I had to hand over the flight controls to the other pilot in order for us to just be safe.

Over time, I ended up waking each day in pain and more tired than when I had gone to bed. I went from doctor to doctor and specialist to specialist, and no one could figure out what was going on with my body. No one seemed to be able to help me.

I was completely exhausted and miserable, yet it didn't cross my mind to leave my job. As a pilot, if you are lucky enough to get a job at a major airline, you don't leave it: You count your lucky stars and stay put until retirement. So, even though my health kept deteriorating, I just kept trying to do my best and soldiered on.

Eventually, I got so sick that I was practically bedridden. I had ups and downs; some things helped, and I'd progress, only to slide back again. This suffering went on for over two decades. I ended up losing so much of what made me feel like me—my fun pastimes and hobbies, most friends faded away, my marriage deteriorated, and I even lost my career as an airline pilot.

On one hand, my marriage eroding and friends falling away happened over time, but on the other hand I had a husband who, while very "busy" with work and who always happened to be out of town on business during birthdays and anniversaries, kept telling me how much he loved me. Right up until the day he told me he was leaving. And no, he was not willing to work on it. And no, he was not willing to go to counseling. He really wasn't willing to do anything. So, from my perspective, I was blindsided. And though he tried to use my illness as an excuse for leaving, I think the actual reason was that he had been hiding money from and cheating on me.

My friendships also suffered. When I was too tired to go to a club, I'd suggest a movie instead, which infuriated my friends; little did they know how hard it was for me to even get out of bed. During this, I felt guilty for always being sick. Over time, I realized it wasn't my fault I was sick or my responsibility to make sure everyone was happy around me. However, I also do not place any blame outside myself. When I look back, I can recognize I did not have the boundaries and self-value that I now carry strongly in my vibration. I attracted the "teachers" I needed to instill these traits in myself. For that, I now hold only gratitude for these people who helped shape my journey.

————◦————

It was the darkest and lowest time of my life. I couldn't work. I couldn't have any fun. I couldn't even really take care of myself. Why was I still here? What was my purpose? I had absolutely no idea.

At my lowest point I realized that, while I was never going to take my own life, I would not be at all upset if it ended right then and there. I just wanted to escape the pain. There was zero joy in being alive, and even worse than that, I felt like I was completely useless to this world. I did not want to experience life like this anymore.

However, there was something that just wouldn't let me give up. I felt a spark in me that wouldn't die. And because of that I just knew there had to be a reason I was still around, and I decided to leave the door slightly ajar for my next step forward.

I was living alone, trying to take care of myself, at which I succeeded some days more than others, but I was still unable to work. My life was filled to the brim with uncertainty and void of security. Then, one day, an email landed in my inbox, and I felt that familiar spark again. A wave of intuition was nudging me, and I took a chance to heed it. I spent three hundred dollars on a course on how to develop my intuition. At that time, three hundred dollars was a ton of money to me, and my fear told me no way should I part with such an amount! But a force inside me inspired me and propelled me to stay with that spark, gently nudging me forward. I pushed past the fear, trusted my intuition, and took a huge and scary leap of faith as I quickly pressed the Buy button and as soon as I did, I felt another spark of excitement. Part of me knew; I was finally taking steps into my new life and into a whole new way of living.

I loved moving deeper into my intuition. I learned everything I could get my hands on about spirituality, consciousness, and energy. All of my forgotten spiritual gifts from childhood came flooding back and then some! I quickly moved into giving intuitive readings for others, then channeling beautiful messages from divine energies and spiritual guides. These helped crack people open to their own empowerment and gifts. I absolutely loved helping people get messages from their guides, hear from their animals, connect with passed loved ones, and even start to tap into their own intuition and spiritual gifts.

I didn't realize what was going on at first, but as I built my business doing readings and channelings, I started gaining back my health, my energy, and my joy. I started to live with passion again. I had purpose in my life, and I KNEW I was where I was meant to be, doing what I was meant to do. Each day reenergized me and brought me joy!

I consistently channeled and downloaded information from my own guidance team. This brought healing, energy shifts, and practices for each stumbling block that appeared in front of me. I began easily seeing patterns of limits and limiting beliefs in myself and in others. With my guides, I learned how to clear them, release them, and live a completely different way. And as a result, I was able to share this transformation by helping others blast right through whatever was holding them back and empower them to live a brand-new life of their dreams as well!

I was doing work I loved. It made so much sense to me that when I finally found and was living my purpose, I was getting my health and energy back. Everything seemed great. I was on my way!

Then it happened.

I started getting sick here or there, and it looked like I might be heading toward a burnout again. I knew the signs and as soon as I saw them, I started getting really scared. I feared the pain of the past and was not wanting to relive it again, ever! I immediately started looking for answers. This time I had the benefit of being well-practiced in letting my intuition lead, and I was led right to Quantum Human Design.

In Quantum Human Design, I found a better way to manage my life. While I was doing what I loved and was meant to be doing, I found there was an even better way of going about it. By learning my unique energetic makeup and operating manual so to speak, pieces of the puzzle began to make sense and fall into place. I had gotten into a strong habit of "efforting" in order to bring success or get myself where I wanted to go, and it had served me really well right up until the point that it didn't, and I would get very sick.

Through Quantum Human Design, I realized I am not meant to make things happen out of my own will and strength, but rather, I am meant to relax and wait for the Universe to give me something to respond to. Whew, that took a load off! I didn't even realize I had always felt like I had to hold the whole world together with only my sheer willpower. For Generators and Manifesting Generators, our way of responding is to get that gut uh-uh or unh-unh response. For us, that response is just natural. Oh, this was becoming so much easier! It was like I was being given a cheat sheet or a key code to life!

As a Manifesting Generator or Time Bender, I am actually energized by having a lot of different things on my plate. It made so much sense! When I had nothing on my plate and no purpose, I was completely miserable. When I found work I loved that brought fulfillment, I rationalized I had found my purpose, I was loving my work, therefore, I should be energized.

But it wasn't what was on my plate, but rather how I was dealing with those things that were de-energizing me. If I was linear and forced myself to finish one thing before starting another, I would be going past the point of my energy for that project, and I would get depleted, which is exactly what happened in my career as a pilot. I efforted trying to stay in a career long after I was meant to leave it because conditioning told me that was what I was supposed to do. That was what a good and responsible person does—the same can be said for my relationships. I always felt I had to put one hundred percent of effort in even when I didn't have the energy to give it and even when the other person wasn't reciprocating because again, that is what a "good person" does. However, I have since found all of this to be backwards.

I realized I would operate better, get more done, and actually feel much better in the long run if I threw out my conditioning and judgment. I needed to stop putting my heart into things that didn't energize me anymore, and release situations that were no longer serving me. I needed to stop forcing. I began to stay with one project until it started to lose my interest, then I would move on to what was piquing my interest. I have come to find my energy doesn't wane nearly as much when I do it that way. Of course, there are times when just playing outside with my dog interests me, or sleep is the only thing on my mind, and then those are things that end up being best for me in those moments. As for relationships: I now know that if what is coming from someone else doesn't feel good for any reason, it's not my signal to fix everything, rather it is my signal to gain some distance and recenter within myself.

The hardest part has been letting go of any preconceived agendas that things should be done a certain way in order to be productive. Especially the old story that we are "flakey" or "flighty" if we just follow our interests all the time. We are all actually much more productive when we work with and honor our Human Design rather than work against it just to align with the conditioning of the outside world. Of course, the end goal is never just productivity. We are meant to enjoy living our lives. Part of that enjoyment will be in learning how we came here to impact the world. But it is oh so important to not get that order reversed and put productivity up on a pedestal where our world's conditioning has it right now. That is exactly backwards. If we strive first and foremost to be productive, we will eventually hit some sort of wall or lose enjoyment. But if we live in our joy every moment, the productivity and impact we are meant to bring to this world will be a natural, easy, and fun byproduct.

You may wonder: Well, this all sounds great, but what about when I have real world deadlines, and have to focus on something beyond my energetic capacity? Great question and that was a great sticking point I had to get through as well.

Even though I had learned a new way of living, I was still twisting myself into a pretzel to fit the demands, schedules, and conditioning of the outer world rather than completely tuning into and living by my own rhythms and varying energies. I was using my spiritual gifts to help others, and I absolutely loved my work, but I was scheduling at times that weren't so good for me or I was forgoing my needs or rest because someone else needed something of me. I still had some learning to do. I had to let go of the fear that others wouldn't be okay if I didn't jump in whenever and wherever. I had to let go of the fear that others wouldn't value me if didn't help them right when they wanted it.

I had to not only learn to let my varying energies and rhythms be okay, but I also needed to respect, honor, and have gratitude for them and let them hold the highest priority spot in my life. Those who respect and value me because of that are in my life and those who don't understand were only ever meant to be temporary teachers directing me back inward to this self-care and love practice.

I am now creating a world that fits my energies rather than trying to force my energy and nature to be something it is not. We think this is impossible when we don't realize that we are all actually creating our realities. It is the inner creating the outer. The outer, responding to the inner. When we fully realize and embody this, we realize how possible it is to create a life, a world where we don't have to change our unique energies, rhythms, or ways of being. In fact, it is for exactly that very uniqueness we are needed here, and part of how we will impact the world.

Do I never get sick anymore, or have I overcome the days where I fear the burnout creeping back in? Nope, I can't say that. But I now fully understand that there are lessons behind each event and circumstance and, truthfully, I have found so many lessons, blessings, and growth in my years of living with illness. I now recognize the arrival of lower energy as a helpful sign to change some aspects of my life rather than a crisis that I need to fight.

I am living a full and fun life now; remembering to orient to joy in most moments. I am making an impact in my own unique way and within my own unique energy and timing. I no longer go into fear if my energy goes lower and instead, I go with it, honor it, and find the beauty in restful and quiet times. As for getting the balance exactly right, well that is a lifelong lesson that we all are continually working on. It's an ongoing process—an ever-changing journey rather than a destination that will be reached and then never worried about again. The ideal balance is a living, and breathing process that looks different in each moment. The best way to find that balance is to create joy. Let the heart and intuition guide to what lights you up. Sometimes that will be rest, sometimes work, and other times play. As long as joy pervades the moment, that is the right balance.

So yes, purpose was part of my answer, but purpose is more than just a vocation and for some it's not a vocation at all. Purpose is partly how we came here to impact the world, but it is also how we live in each moment. Are we living in a way that brings us to joy? If so, then we are living in our purpose and are on our purpose path. Purpose is expressed and lives through each moment. And just like the ideal balance, rather than it being a destination or fixed point, purpose is a process and a journey that is ever evolving just as we are ever evolving on this human journey we call life!

We are here to enjoy the process, the evolvement. Life is meant to be our own creation of joy. We are here to enjoy the ride. And yep, just like any rollercoaster ride, there are ups and downs but if even from the dips, we still continually search for what brings us to joy in each moment, we will never get lost.

I followed the nudges of my heart at many points in my life and now I do so all the time. Those nudges led me into being a pilot which was a dream career for a period of my life. It also led me to move to Hawaii and find my childhood dream of living in the magical mountains on the beach. It has led me to a second dream career of helping others with my spiritual gifts and hopefully making the world just a little bit brighter as I shine my light of joy.

I have experienced through my own journey and through guiding others on theirs that when the conventional is turned on its head and we allow the heart to lead, it finds joy. Living in joy naturally leads to living out our purpose and impact. When living in joy, we will discover that those impossible dreams manifest before our very eyes.

You too can make the impossible possible when you are living in joy and loving your evolving purpose every day.

Lisa Robinett

Certified Quantum Human Design Specialist,
Certified Akashic Records Reader,
Certified Intuitive Reader and Spiritual Coach,
and Certified Animal Communicator

5/1 Time Bender (Manifesting Generator)

Lisa Robinett spent the majority of her career life as a commercial airline captain flying Boeing 737s across the Pacific. Following some transformative life events that assisted her spiritual awakening, she is now a professional intuitive, channel, Quantum Human Design Specialist, and spiritual coach.

Lisa's mission is to help humanity realize that the natural state is one of joy and to ignite others to live their highest most joy-filled life, purpose, and path. She is here to help us remember that we are all divine spiritual beings with our own unique spiritual gifts and that we are meant to live with connection and meaning as well as joy and bliss.

Living a life connected with nature in Hawaii, Lisa joyfully resides with her two kitties and border collie puppy, Brynn. She also enjoys her work as a professional animal communicator. In her spare time, she loves playing and relaxing at the beach, hiking, gardening, photography, and learning anything and everything. She is currently working toward her PhD in metaphysics from the University of Sedona specializing in Conscious-Centered Living.

She uses her spiritual gifts to teach lightworkers how to discover their own unique spiritual gifts, get clear on their higher purpose, and break through the fears and limits that have been holding them back. With these teachings, she encourages her students so that they can go out and start helping people while also making a living using their gifts and living their purpose.

You can find out more and connect at:

LisaRobinett.com

Mind and Body Connection:
The Science of Joy

By Caroline M. Sabbah

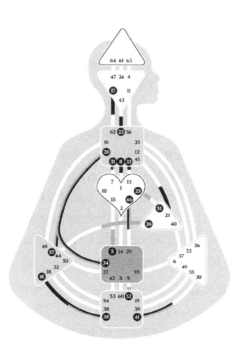

Caroline M. Sabbah's Human Design Chart

Cultivating Joy is the first step to nurturing lifelong resilience and reconnecting with yourself, your purpose, and your inner medicine which makes the lifelong journey towards health and well-being more easeful.

What if it were that simple?

Finding Purpose Through Joy

My purpose by design is Joy. Yes, literally Joy. My role is to identify, call out, and correct patterns that prevent joy in myself and others. Being joyful is an essential part of our natural state.

When I finally allowed myself to reconnect with my joy, my inner wisdom and medicine reconciled the dualities within, allowing the lost parts of myself to be reclaimed. With this, my purpose became clear: Empower women with knowledge and understanding of who they are, and how their minds and bodies work; help them reconnect mind, body, soul, and inner medicine to become who they want to be; aid and assist them to unlock their health and well-being to its greatest potential.

Cultivating joy is the first step toward that journey into our inner medicine and towards integrity of self. Unfortunately, many of us have lost our ancestral teachings, stories, and roots. We forgot parts of ourselves. With life challenges, loss, illness, pain, and suffering, we often disconnect further from our bodies, our minds, and our souls to survive, losing our joy and wonder in the process.

The tipping point in my story began at age twenty-eight, working twelve-hour-plus days as a litigator when I became pregnant. At twenty-six weeks, I started preterm contractions. At twenty-seven weeks, my water broke. I was terrified for our son. December 17th, 2000 was not only the scariest day but also one of the most precious days of my life; I gave birth at thirty weeks to a beautiful three-and-a-half-pound baby boy. A few months after our son's birth, my husband was offered an opportunity in Manhattan. We were young, and I think we saw it as a chance for a new beginning.

Nine months later, only a few days after our baby boy was taken off his heart monitor, we—excited and exhausted—moved to Manhattan. That was August 1st, 2001. On September 11, 2001, the second scariest day of our lives happened, 9/11. Thankfully my husband was working in Midtown and not in the Towers. After a quick call from my husband letting me know he was safe, I witnessed, from our balcony, the fall of the first tower. I held my baby in my arms and watched the cloud of debris making its way through the New York City skyline. When I look back, I see how the compounding effect of our son's premature birth and 9/11 impacted both our physical and emotional well-being.

We decided to move back home to Canada. I couldn't return to twelve-hour days, so I pivoted from litigation to mediation. Worst idea ever. Not only did I then deal with conflict head-on, but I was also the sounding board of all that conflict. My health deteriorated. With the knowledge I now have of my genetics and Human Design, I understand why that was.

In 2003, I caught an unknown virus in the Dominican Republic and ended up in the emergency room with pericarditis, unable to breathe. My health declined rapidly afterward. I lost my zest for life, my joy. I was exhausted and in deep, physical pain. I couldn't think. I couldn't function. I couldn't remember names. I couldn't remember dates and events. I couldn't sleep.

I didn't realize that all of my body's cells were tallying the trauma we had lived through and that was the reason it no longer had the resiliency to fight off the viruses. My body was in constant stress mode, my mind hypervigilant. My barrel was overflowing. The burden on my immune system and the maladaptive stress response were too much; the stage was set for chronic inflammation.

I clearly remember a day I'd picked our son up from daycare. I was driving home, completely exhausted when it hit me—I couldn't remember where we lived or what side of the road I was supposed to drive on. All I remember was looking into my rear-view mirror at my son and being terrified. At that moment, I felt utterly betrayed by both my body and mind and their inability to keep us safe.

I knew things had to change. I needed answers, and I needed to get better. It took years to get a diagnosis, but I *chose* to get better.

In retrospect I understand that changing my outlook helped me make better choices and develop better habits, including nutrition and lifestyle, which slowly improved my health.

If only one change could be made right now, I believe cultivating joy would be the most impactful towards better health and well-being; the quality of one's choices would improve making the journey towards health and well-being more easeful. In fact, the Dalai Lama stated that joy has an epigenetic power called "Mental Immunity" to protect against stress-related health issues.

Later on, armed with the knowledge of my genetics, my Human Design, the science of neuroplasticity and epigenetics, and the clear understanding that I have the power of choice, I chose to cultivate joy and reconnect with my mind, body, and soul, *and* my inner medicine.

Easeful is not easy. I still catch myself in moments of high stress, defaulting to old habits of letting fears permeate my choices and allowing maladaptive stress responses to take over. It's a practice, and it doesn't need to be perfect. In fact, the more you chase happiness, the more fleeting it is. Joy is inside us; it is our birthright and often appears when we let go and surrender into just being, putting our thoughts to rest. Healing isn't linear, it's a beautiful dance between awareness, choice, and change.

Today I am more resilient and when I find myself faced with emotional, health, or stress challenges, I can pivot more easefully back to better health and well-being.

The Science of Joy

Research shows how living with purpose can improve our health markers and how cultivating joy can improve our health and well-being.

But what is joy? Joy and happiness are often used interchangeably; however, happiness is a broad and long-term evaluation of our lives. Happiness also relies on external factors while *joy* is a state of mind that leads to a life of satisfaction and meaning.

Joy might seem like a frivolous objective, but it is not a luxury; it doesn't need to be earned. It is *inside* all of us. It is medicine.

We are in an epidemic of exhaustion and burnout, inflammation, overwhelm, anxiety, disconnect, and seriousness. Many live in constant hypervigilance and constant stress like I did after my son's premature birth, 9/11, and professional shifts. Many feel a need for change but are stuck.

Why not begin by cultivating physical, emotional, mental, and spiritual resilience by manifesting more joy, tapping into the inner wisdom of our body with *joy medicine*?

We must reconnect, come out of our survival states, and start feeling again. Joy is not about *avoiding* negative feelings but about allowing feelings to happen. We must *allow* emotions to move through us and to observe them, understanding that these feelings do not define us (i.e., not I *am* angry but rather, I *feel* angry). It is important to understand that real joy is not materialistic; it is consciously intended within. It's not our circumstances that need to change but our mindsets.

To initiate the shift, start by focusing on life's simple, beautiful joys like the wind in the leaves, the laughter of a baby, a hug, or a smile, and slowly build from there. One step at a time. The more these moments are embraced, the more they will appear.

These changes require conscious awareness, so by choosing a different perspective, it is possible to cultivate joy in our everyday circumstances. Choice breeds change and change happens slowly and on many levels. What does your mind need? What does your soul need? What does your body need?

Mental and emotional well-being are connected to physical well-being. There's a bidirectional relationship between thoughts, emotions, and physical health on mental health and mood. Stress, shame, and trauma stored in cells trigger hypervigilant inflammatory responses from the nervous system. The gut is where most of the immune system lies. Hormones and neurotransmitters often color how the world is perceived and seen.

Homeostasis is the process by which the body actively maintains balance to survive. When we get sick, the body will strive for homeostasis—the body's inner wisdom. The body communicates with symptoms (pain, dis-ease, etc.). By deepening the mind-body connection, we support returning to homeostasis, to self-healing, and to unlocking our health and well-being potential. However, we as humans have disconnected from our bodies, mostly living in our minds, ignoring, avoiding, or suppressing our body's messages. As Human Design teaches, the mind is not meant to make choices or decisions, yet most of us *are* ruled by our minds and are disconnected from our body's innate wisdom.

Advances in neuroplasticity inform us that we can change our brains and create new neural pathways. Addressing our thoughts and habits are important when looking to improve resilience, health, and well-being to influence our genetics. Both the body and the mind need the other to be healthy, and Human Design is an incredible opportunity into the study of self and non-self.

Recent advances in genetics provide insight into how genes function. Our unique genetic blueprints allow us to understand ourselves, enables us to take responsibility for our health and to make conscious decisions that can positively influence our bodies and minds. It's a foundation; a critical roadmap with valuable insights.

Does this sound familiar? Human Design also provides the unique roadmap necessary to gain valuable insights into personality, health, decision-making, life path, and energetic experiences, which guides us to living authentically and with integrity.

When you look at genetics and Human Design, they both inform us of the opportunity to self-actualize, to understand our uniqueness, to receive the gift of inner autonomy, and to take radical responsibility for our health and well-being. When we trust our own inner wisdom and medicine and when we cultivate joy to gain lifelong resilience and reclaim our purpose, we move away from confusion, overwhelm, anxiety, and stress. When we do this, we move toward the highest expression of our genetics and Design.

The science of epigenetics (*epi* means above the gene) provides insight into how our lifestyles, experiences, and choices impact our genetic expression. It's a paradigm shift that moves us from being genetic victims to a place of self-empowerment.

Our daily choices—nutrition, stress-management, environment, lifestyle, energy, choices, beliefs, and perceptions—about life have the potential to determine gene expression. Mindset does matter. Our genetics and epigenetics—the physical plane—with Human Design—the energetic plane—make us who we are. The practices of health and well-being and how we understand ourselves are rapidly evolving. Understanding that Human Design is our life and soul blueprint exemplifies the epitome of epigenetics. And it's that knowledge which energetically influences our genes toward infinite potential.

While both these modalities can help us shift and heal, they can also work against us if we come from a place of fear and conditioning. Letting fear, old patterns, and beliefs govern our choices can damage our health. Seeing them as opportunities for growth gives us the power to influence our genetic expression.

The science of psychoneuroimmunology coined by Robert Adler, is a subfield of psychosomatic medicine that studies how the immune system and the nervous system interact and how psychological stress makes us more susceptible to illnesses. It specifically studies the connection between the brain (thoughts and moods) and the immune system (disease and healing).

While many studies focus on how stress and certain negative emotions impact the immune system and premature aging, studies also demonstrate the benefits of happiness or positive emotions on health and well-being.

As noted, symptoms are the way our bodies tell us something is out of balance. Many of us ignore these symptoms, which leads to a greater mind/body disconnect. For example, you may try to ignore pain, but that doesn't make it go away. Pain comes from different sources and once we understand that our emotions are stored in our cells, we can investigate what our cells might be holding on to and what the pain is trying to convey. Another example is unresolved trauma trapped in the body. During times of high stress, as in a traumatic event, the nervous system acts to keep the body safe. Each time the stress response is activated, the nervous system "remembers" what it did before to keep safe and activates a cascade of neurotransmitters and chemicals throughout the body. Over time, that response becomes maladaptive if every stressor, big and small, excite the same reaction.

Basic internet research shows that little moments of joy can help the body recover from the effects of stress and can help us find meaning and purpose in difficult circumstances. Little moments that *I* allowed into my life—and cultivated—helped me restore my emotional and physical resources that had become depleted and allowed me to become more resilient in challenging moments. We are able to learn these new coping mechanisms through neuroplasticity, which is the ability of neurons to change their function, chemical profile, or structure. We can never unlearn anything; rather, we create new pathways and strengthen them with practice. Neurons that wire together, fire together. Where focus goes, energy flows. Resilience builds resilience. Joy builds joy.

Choosing joy builds a life of purpose and resilience allowing us to pivot to overcome life's challenges and helps us support our long-term health, resilience, vitality, and well-being.

When we maintain a high level of purposeful living it correlates with better health behavior but also with healthier gene expression, longevity, reduced metabolic dysregulation, and fewer diseases.

The Genetics of Joy

There are genetic traits that make us more joyful but, as you now know, genetics can be influenced. Joy has the epigenetic power to protect against stress-related health issues.

Psychologist Sonja Lyubomirsky in *The How of Happiness* suggests that 50 percent of happiness is determined by genetic factors. The other 50 percent is determined by a combination of circumstances. According to Lyubomirsky, some factors that seem to have the greatest influence on increasing our happiness are our ability to reframe our situation more positively, our ability to experience gratitude, and our choice to be kind and generous (2007, Penguin Books, p. 20-22).

Joy by Design

Genetics, epigenetics, and Human Design empower our choices. An open center is an opportunity for wisdom while a defined center is for more certainty and consistency. The same applies to the gates and channels. Remember you have *all* of the chart. We all do. The only difference is what energy is consistently available to you and about learning how to use undefined energy wisely. You can rewrite your story. You are free to choose who you want to be and how you want to experience your life.

Joy is an innate part of all of us. An innate part of our Design as human beings.

Most of you have experienced the state of *being* in moments when you experienced a deep inner state of ease, peace, and flow in the joy zone. We can experience that state in a variety of ways. Allowing ourselves the joy to simply *be* can impact our well-being and reconnect us to our inner wisdom. Also, bringing play back into our lives is a great catalyst towards joy. Play with your Design. Experiment. Have fun with it. There's nothing negative in our unique designs, only infinite opportunities and possibilities into our potential for joy, vitality, health and well-being.

When we tap into our Type, we find the gift of inner guidance, an internal barometer helping us identify if we are in alignment with our Design. When we first discover our Human Design blueprint, we often get a confirmation of our intuitive gifts. I find my clients experience the same feeling when we review their genetic tests. It gives us permission to trust in our inner wisdom and medicine. Human Design, like genetics, is a light guiding us towards exploration, providing us with guideposts and insights. This understanding and gift for acceptance allows us to sit in self-empowerment and let go of old limiting beliefs, conditioning, and patterns.

The exploration of your Design in itself holds so much potential for cultivating joy and vitality. The ultimate source of a happy life is internal, inside all of us.

Too often we try to bring change through willpower, which is largely unsustainable since only 37 percent of the population has consistent access to willpower energy. If you have an open or undefined Will/Ego/Heart Center, the energy of willpower is simply not available to you consistently. We so often fall into the trap of guilt and shame of not being able to implement long-lasting change. While understanding the cultivation of joy, shifting towards a positive mindset helps us make these changes more easefully without relying on pure willpower.

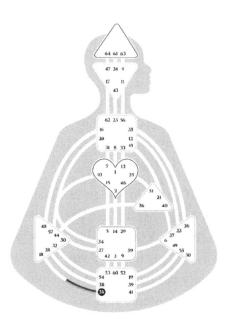

We can't talk about joy without exploring Gate 58, the gate with the potential for joy and vitality. Gate 58 is part of my life's purpose. It is worth looking into whether you have this gate or not. With Gate 58, we carry the love of life within us and a deep trust and understanding of the good in life, and with this joyful spark we may inspire others and may carry the ability to see what needs to be explored by ourselves and others in order to experience more joy and vitality.

This gate also reminds us that joy comes from the inside, and that we must embrace all facets of emotions to be able to experience joy. It's time to embrace simple things. Simply appreciating being alive helps us cultivate joy.

I propose a three-prong approach to cultivating joy. Bring your childlike curiosity and sense of play to the table and be open to new perspectives. Playfulness is a necessary part of our learning, growth, and evolution.

1. Reset Your Rhythm—Create Space

You need space to cultivate joy and space to be present. How can you create space and more time in your life to allow yourself to slow down and respect your rhythms, your cycles, and *be,* not *do,* according to your Design?

Write down everything that takes up your time. Run through your days and write it all down. Do it as an observer; don't identify with it. You do not want to create overwhelm—quite the contrary—you want to be able to be creative and come up with new possibilities and solutions.

Now it's time to play and be creative. What can be taken off your schedule, what is no longer needed, what can you delegate, what can be simplified, automated? Once you have more space available, you will have more time to cultivate the things that bring you joy which will be explored further in 3: Reclaim Your Joy.

When you do not allow yourself space to integrate, space to build new habits, and space to contemplate, you are riding a whirlwind. The busier you are the clearer you need to be about where you spend your energy. You must be clearer about your boundaries. As you cannot address the body in isolation, nor can you do it with your mind and soul. By creating space and time and truly connecting to your rhythm, your right timing, and your energy, you can dive into the action steps. It is easy to forget sleep has a specific rhythm which include our hormones, the seasons, the days. Tap back into your natural rhythm.

Create a schedule that permits sufficient time for rest and play and that allows you to cultivate joy.

2. Reconnect to Your Heart

This exercise works to open the Heart Center and reconnect with the self—the soul—by bringing the nervous system into a coherent and resilient state. When you consciously intend to be joyful, you start shifting your perspective. Changes begin to take place in your body and your mind. As your slowly learn to choose actions and situations that align you with your intention and purpose, the momentum of positive change starts to grow. By doing an activity repetitively, it will start changing the structure of the brain creating new neural pathways. Even just imagining the activity over and over has an impact on neural structure. By actively imagining feelings of joy or recalling joyful experiences, you can help to make changes in your brain that can bring more joy into your life.

This exercise is partially based on the HeartMath Institute's techniques. You can find impactful resources and practices as well as more in-depth explanations on their website.

Step 1: Find a quiet and comfortable place to sit. Place your hands on your heart and take several deep belly breaths, imagining that you are opening up your Heart Center and releasing all of your tension out through your mouth. Take deep, comfortable inhales through the nose, expanding your belly and opening your Heart Center, and then releasing all through the mouth. Continue for a few breaths until you feel relaxed and grounded.

Step 2: Now, close your eyes if that feels comfortable and safe for you, and remember a joyful memory while you continue to breathe comfortably through your heart. It can be a moment when you felt content, at peace, or in flow, such as a walk by the beach, in a forest, or a precious moment with a loved one or pet. Sometimes when we are in pain, it is really hard to recall these moments; in that case, simply remember something you are grateful for. Start there.

Step 3: Next, remember it through all of your senses. What does it feel like, look like, sound like, and smell like? Let that joy flow from your heart and expand through every inch of your body allowing that reconnection with the heart and the body. Once there, in that state, if you wish, you can visualize your intention for meditating, or focus on your health goals.

Practice regularly and this will become easier and more effective. Allow at least five minutes and if you feel like it, extend the time slowly to what feels most beneficial to you.

3. Reclaim Your Joy

Now that you've created space, reconnected with your heart and inner wisdom and medicine, how can you reclaim your joy? Grab a pen and a journal, make time and space for this next exercise, practice the heart breathing exercise above, settle into your body, into your heart, and then ask yourself the following questions:

- What brings me joy? Make a list, but don't attach it to a job, a career, or life path; don't try to rationalize it or find the *how* you will bring it to life, simply focus on just the *what*.
- Time to play. When you remember the power of play, it acts as a catalyst to your joy and is an essential part of your healing. Begin to explore your list within the context of your Design and have fun with it, play with it, bring in curiosity, imagination, and wonder. Open up to possibilities. What if joy became part of my daily experience? What would that feel like, look like? How can I cultivate joy with my thoughts, beliefs, and actions? How can I begin to cultivate more joy today and a gratitude practice into my life?

The how and the when will come when the time is right and according to your Type, your Authority, and your Strategy.

Once you become aware of joy and cultivate your joy, you will reconnect with your purpose. On your journey, remember that you need to begin where you are and see the good that is in your life now. It doesn't mean that you can't intend for change and more, but you do need to start with seeing the good in what you have, by slowly shifting your perception.

Joy and gratitude go hand in hand. We think joy lives in the extraordinary but it's in the ordinary little things in life. When you open up to the gratitude of these little things, you open up to joy. Play with the steps, first open up space, then your heart, and then reconnect with what brings you joy.

We all have an internal cry for joy. We need to go inward and reconnect with ourselves to rewire some neural pathways and then we can truly implement changes in an easeful manner without solely relying on our Will Center (which in the end can only bring us so far).

Remember, how we react to life can be in our control. While we may not control what happens *to* us, we can still choose how we react to it. We can all fall into patterns of negative thinking when under stress or during difficult circumstances, so be kind and gentle with yourself.

My last insight to you is to reconnect with self and dive inside into your inner knowing. Living out of alignment and integrity can be an underlying root cause of disease, exhaustion, and pain. We must clear our old patterns, beliefs, habits, lifestyle, and environment that block or limit our ability to step into our health and well-being potential, and into the person we were meant to be.

Both Human Design and genetics are tools that can empower and guide you into this journey of reconnection with yourself; releasing maladaptive responses, habits, and patterns you are holding on to in your body, reclaiming your inner medicine. When you understand who you are, what you are here to do, know and understand how your body functions, and how to support its highest expression, you can start living in integrity and alignment with your physical, emotional, mental, and spiritual bodies, bringing you joy, vitality, purpose, and lifelong resilience.

Caroline M. Sabbah

LLL (Law), CNP, ACC,
Functional Nutritionist, and Coach

1/4 Time Bender (Manifesting Generator)

Caroline combines functional nutrition, the science of nutritional genomics (genetics/DNA testing), and Human Design for greater women's health and well-being. She addresses women as a whole, from the gut to the brain, from the heart to the mind, and all that is in between.

Caroline's core mission is to empower women with the knowledge and understanding of how their unique mind and body work with the insight of genetics and Human Design. Recognizing these connections will guide them towards their potential for health and well-being and help them reconnect with their inner medicine.

Caroline started her career path as a litigation lawyer and mediator and is no stranger to high stress and chronic health issues as she went through her own struggles with chronic disease. She lives in Toronto, Canada with her two wonderful children who fill her heart with joy and her loving and supporting husband. They have two crazy dogs and a Guinea pig that light up their days. She is a caregiver to her adoring mother with Alzheimer's disease. This role has given her a firsthand understanding of the fear of losing oneself. Her fuel for her mission of empowering women with their health and well-being is through the lessons she has learned in caring for her mother and in navigating her own health. In her free time, if she's not reading or learning something new, you'll find her walking, hiking, biking, or skiing in nature, or in her other joyful place, a tennis court.

If you feel called to dive deeper into the science of you and explore your health and well-being potential with a personalized approach, informed by you and designed with genetic insight, visit Caroline's website at:

carolinemsabbah.com

Follow Caroline on Instagram @carolinemsabbah
or Linkedin.com/in/caroline-m-sabbah-a0769618

When I Stopped Chasing Success, Purpose Found Me

By Corissa Stepp

Appearances aren't always what they seem. We have come to understand this in our digitized age of social media where a photo of a happy family doesn't always indicate that everything is copacetic at home. I know this was true for me.

From an outside perspective, I had it all—a beautiful home, a happy family, good health, and comfortable access to resources and creature comforts. Behind the curtain, however, I was slowly falling apart, too afraid to ask for help because it would mean I was weak or incapable. Yes, I was grateful for all I had and for my comfortable lifestyle, but what people couldn't perceive was the gaping hole of loneliness and disconnection I was hiding. I felt lost and struggled for purpose and meaning.

I hadn't always felt this way. In my twenties, before marriage and having children, I thought I had found my purpose. I had a career in finance, working for some of the world's best investment banks and hedge funds, and I felt that being challenged mentally was stimulating. A six-figure salary at the tender age of twenty-four was an accomplishment. Buying my first place by twenty-five and then a condo in the Hamptons before I turned twenty-nine was like hitting the "success" lottery. And it was easy. I was a high achiever and derived a lot of value from doing well in my career.

My definition of success changed once I became a mother in my thirties. Provided my boys ate, slept, and hit their milestones on time or ahead of schedule, I felt I was doing a pretty good job at the mom gig; however, as my boys grew older, I needed more intellectual stimulation and adult interaction.

When my boys were two and four, I was offered an opportunity to work for a former hedge fund client in business development. It was exciting! The idea of reclaiming my old self was alluring and exhilarating. Being able to drink a steaming hot latte while sitting in my office and having stimulating conversations with clients and colleagues was extremely appealing. I said yes to the opportunity even though not being home with my boys was heartbreaking.

Every weekday morning at 6:15 AM, Esther, our nanny, would arrive before the kids woke so that I could make the 6:35 AM bus. On the days when my youngest did wake up before I left, I would kiss him goodbye and quickly scoot out the door before he devolved into a full-blown tantrum, screaming and crying, "Mommy!!! Mommy!!! Don't go!! Don't leave!" It broke my heart every time, and there were many mornings when I drove to the bus, blinded by the tears stinging my eyes.

There were also countless mornings when I wouldn't see my boys before I left the house. I would call home on my walk from the Port Authority Bus Terminal to my office on Park Ave, across from the Waldorf Astoria, to say good morning. Those calls were not much easier as my boys would often cry, whine, and beg me to come home or ask when I was coming home. It slowly killed me, especially knowing that I wouldn't get home until just before their bedtime at 7:30 PM. During this time, my husband was also commuting to NYC, so our kids spent more time with strangers than with their parents. This is not an anomaly for many working parents, but after nine months, it became clear one January morning that this scenario was not sustainable.

Sitting across the breakfast table from Tyler, who was only five years old, I noticed his ear looked wildly discolored. It was *purple*! Deeply concerned, I questioned him about it. He looked up, afraid to answer. I had to find out what happened—it looked painful! I asked him a series of yes or no questions.

"Did you hit your head?"

"No."

"Did your brother hit you with something?"

"No."

"Did something happen at school?"

He slowly shook his head back and forth and looked down.

I began to get frustrated, and then something clicked.

Gently, I asked, "Did Esther do that to your ear?"

He hesitated and looked scared. "I didn't mean to," he whined, "I wasn't going to hurt Everett! I was just mad that he took my Iron Man!"

My head spun. I thought I was going to throw up. How could the woman I trusted, who had quickly become a part of our family, do this to my child?

I had to do damage control. My sweet child thought it was his fault that the nanny put her hands on him! I wanted to scream, call her, and demand answers.

Instead, I pulled Tyler into my arms and explained that no matter how he was behaving, it was not okay for Esther or anyone to ever put their hands on him, especially not in a way that really hurt.

The relief that washed over his face once he understood he wasn't the one in trouble and wasn't going to be blamed for what had happened, was bittersweet. He hugged me tightly and told me it wasn't the first time. She often twisted his ear when he wasn't behaving, and she did other things that were very frightening to my three and five-year-old sons.

For nearly nine months, Esther had been part of our family, spending over twelve hours a day with my children most days. She seemingly cared about them, and we cared about her, giving her generous birthday and Christmas gifts, paid time off, and other perks.

I was heartbroken by this betrayal. The situation made me feel deeply ashamed and guilty. Suddenly, working and rediscovering my identity through my previous career felt shallow, selfish, and misaligned.

I tried for six weeks to find a replacement after Esther was fired but trusting someone with our boys was difficult. We made a family decision—I resigned from my job.

At first, I was happy being home again with my boys, relishing in the mundane tasks of maintaining our house, attending and volunteering at school events, and doing all the cooking, cleaning, and caretaking. My husband was still working long hours, but I was home with our boys, which made us all feel much safer.

When the boys went to elementary school, that nagging feeling of needing and wanting more and feeling less and less fulfilled settled back in. I struggled to find purpose and meaning. My roles as a wife and mother appeased my need to people-please and overachieve as a perfectionist, but soon I realized I'd lost my sense of self in the process.

When I looked in the mirror, I stopped recognizing the face staring back at me. My eyes looked dead. The once happy, optimistic girl I had been was bitter, resentful, and chronically frustrated. I was stuck in a hole so deep and wide that I couldn't find my way out.

In my desperate search to remember who I was, I scrolled through old photos on my phone to see when I had lost that sparkle in my eye. When had I truly lost myself? Did I ever really know who I was?

It occurred to me that no one knew the real me—I'd spent my whole life trying to fit into the boxes other people defined for me. I didn't feel safe being me and instead, blended into the background because I felt I didn't fit in anywhere.

I knew I should've been grateful—I didn't have to work, and I could be home with my children, but it wasn't enough.

This all came to a head when a dear friend was diagnosed with terminal metastatic breast cancer at forty-one. As she ran out of time, I questioned everything. I had time to make different choices and change the aspects I wasn't happy with.

As my friend's light in the world dimmed, a fire was lit within me to figure out what was "wrong" with me and to discover my purpose and meaning because they weren't just going to land in my lap.

I sought and luckily found a myriad of tools and modalities to help me rediscover myself. First, I learned to meditate, and soon I began to open up to a different vibration. On days I skipped my meditation, I had less patience. My kids used to yell at me to meditate when they saw me getting worked up; even *they* saw the difference in how I responded to them.

Sitting in stillness allowed some fascinating insights to come to light. I'd hit a wall professionally and personally. In the past, I'd filled the holes within me through my career and my family, and by overachieving and satisfying others. However, I'd fallen short. I felt unfulfilled, overwhelmed, stressed, and constantly exhausted. Deep down I was very unhappy, and my soul was tired of living life at the surface. I needed more.

More what though? I wasn't sure. All I knew was that something was missing, leaving me desperate to find the missing pieces.

In this search for my truth, I booked a session with an intuitive, a woman who was clairvoyant. I was skeptical that she would have the answers I sought, but I left the session with my mind blown. She seemingly knew so much about me and could clearly articulate what I hadn't yet been able to put into words. In the end, she said the most curious thing: "Your guides are insisting that I tell you about this thing called Human Design. I don't know much about it as I've only recently heard about it, but they are adamant you check it out."

Little did she or I know in that moment just how much that last little piece of advice would impact my life. As soon as our session ended, I searched Human Design on my phone. The first link was an invitation to download my chart, and as soon as it loaded, chills ran up and down my arms and neck. I would later come to recognize this sensation as a sign from my guides that I was on the right track or that I'd encountered a profound truth. The shapes, colors, and lines of my chart didn't make sense right away, but over time, my insatiable quest for purpose and meaning was satisfied.

One of the first things I learned about Human Design was my Type. I am a Generator and one of the first principles I understood was that just because I have the energy and capacity to do all the things, doesn't mean I have to. This idea was incredibly liberating, especially to an overachiever and people pleaser. Realizing I could let go of the guilt of always doing and instead, I could follow my joy made me feel like I was six years old again and was being asked what I wanted to be when I grew up! I felt empowered knowing I had "permission" to choose from a whole array of possibilities, that I could break out of the box I'd been confined to my whole life. I no longer had to meet anyone else's expectations but my own. I'm here to do the things that light me up and devote myself to those opportunities that feel right and aligned. It still amazes me that it took me a little over forty years to realize this!

This realization allowed me to play with the possibilities of what my life's next chapter would look like. I explored the idea of becoming a coach so I could help other women get unstuck and embrace a life they deeply craved while helping them transform their relationships into deep and meaningful connections.

Human Design helped me better understand my natural talents and gifts, allowing me to lean into and embrace them. As a 2nd Line Profile, it was hard to know what I was naturally good at since the 2nd Line is often unaware of the things that come easily to them. They tend to assume that what is easy for them is easy for everyone else as well. Being able to see what I was actually good at in my chart was reassuring and validating.

With a 2nd Line Profile, I was naturally perceptive and picked things up quickly. As a result, in my career, my managers often put more responsibility on my plate, believing I could handle anything they threw at me. Whenever they increased my responsibilities, I cheerily said yes because I felt I had to prove my worth. I felt guilty saying no because I knew I was capable of getting the task done and exceeding their expectations; however, overcommitting depleted me. I was drowning, and my struggle to stay afloat burned me out. I'd always proudly been a serial people pleaser and perfectionist, never recognizing how unhealthy it was until I learned more about my patterns through the lens of Human Design.

Studying Quantum Human Design and learning EFT (emotional freedom techniques) through Karen Curry Parker's Quantum Alignment System helped me break the patterns of people-pleasing by rewriting my self-limiting beliefs, learning to fully love and accept myself, and value the person that I am, not the person I thought I had to be. I finally learned how to set and maintain clear, strong, and healthy boundaries, and I stopped committing to things that didn't excite me. I've learned to honor my time, my energy, my authenticity, and my value. I no longer willingly hand my power over to others and I prioritize my needs and well-being so that I can be a better mother, partner, daughter, and friend.

My open Solar Plexus leaves me susceptible to engaging in people-pleasing and co-dependent behaviors. When the emotions of those closest to me are intense or negative, I absorb and amplify those emotions, which feels wildly uncomfortable. In the past, I responded by numbing myself emotionally and compromising my needs to keep everyone else happy because it was more manageable. Realizing that I had shut down one of my greatest superpowers of being able to attune intuitively to others 'feelings was sad and disappointing. How had I shut down one of my greatest gifts?

Through deep reflection, I realized that I had been slowly shutting down my emotions since I was a teenager. In high school, I was seen as the strong one; I rarely cried, didn't get overly emotional, and did my best to avoid drama. It wasn't that I was unemotional—I was just trying not to take on the intense emotions of those around me.

My perfectionistic tendencies were born out of my belief that I had to "perform and be perfect" to make others happy and to receive the love and attention I craved. I believed that if I could control my outer environment, my inner world would be safe. If I made others happy, they wouldn't reject me. If I pushed myself harder and harder in school and in my relationships, then I wouldn't fail, make a mistake, or disappoint anyone. Keeping this up was exhausting.

By the time I got to college, I was unwittingly burned out. My major didn't allow me to ease up because I chose to challenge myself with a degree in quantitative finance (akin to financial engineering). I couldn't stop there. I turned one of my minors into a second major in financial economics. By senior year, I couldn't pursue just any investment bank—I had to fight for a job at one of the top investment banks. My people-pleasing, perfectionist, and control-freak tendencies pushed me to success. No wonder I had been so proud of these "traits"—until I realized how toxic they were!

Once I became a mother and quit my career, my control-freak, people-pleasing, and perfectionistic tendencies were no longer valued, and that's when resentment kicked in. I was no longer recognized or appreciated for my efforts, so instead of allowing myself to feel the weight of what that meant, that I felt I was unworthy of love and attention, I stopped feeling the world around me almost entirely. Deep within, I thought I was disappointing everyone around me and that felt too painful. It'd been easier to put up walls and distract myself by chasing the next shiny gold object.

Learning more about the dynamics of how energy flows through the Solar Plexus, I became more discerning about which emotions were mine and which were not. I learned how to protect my energy from the intense emotional waves of others. This has been a game-changer because now I set boundaries that make it safe to feel my emotions and to let go of emotions that aren't mine. I limit my exposure to people who create drama or intense situations out of a need for attention. I can see through what's being said or the fear that is sponsoring the behavior and see a different perspective. When I stay calm and centered and listen to what's going on, I can empathize and provide more support lovingly and compassionately rather than getting myself worked up and ending up in the same heightened state my loved ones are in. This has been a big lesson because I live with three Manifesting Generators, and their emotional themes are anger and frustration. When I'm angry, I ask if it's my anger or someone else's. If it's mine, it sticks around a bit longer and begs me to honor it so it can share its wisdom. If it's someone else's, it quickly dissipates, and I can literally "shake it off" (thanks, Taylor Swift!) by moving my body or belting out one of my favorite tunes.

Being able to discern this difference has helped to improve not only my emotional health and well-being but also my relationships with my children and loved ones. I can now safely access and express my feelings. The pandemic, in retrospect, highlighted why it was so hard for me to spend so much time constantly surrounded by my loved ones. I struggled with being immersed in the intense emotional energy of my emotionally defined son and his father. Needing time away to discharge their emotional energy, in conjunction with my 2nd Line Profile, I often felt the need to withdraw and be alone. At least a couple days a week, I would escape and drive around aimlessly, or I'd sit alone in a parking lot and journal. I felt very guilty about it at the time. After all, we were all struggling, and I felt like I was selfishly abandoning my family to stay sane.

Once I understood that I needed more alone time to discharge the emotional energy I absorb and amplify, in conjunction with my need to hermit, I felt validated and free to take time away when I needed it to restore and recharge my battery. Now, when things get too intense, I take a deep breath, discern whose emotions I am picking up on, and calmly respond.

I also discovered my purpose. As I fell deeper down the rabbit hole, I knew I wanted to help women heal their wounds, let go of their self-limiting beliefs, and ditch the people-pleasing. Experiencing the power and transformation of using the Quantum Alignment System, I knew it would be one of the modalities I'd use with my clients to help them achieve meaningful shifts in their lives. I receive great joy and fulfillment in helping other women reconnect with their authenticity, purpose, and worthiness.

Learning how to listen to my Sacral and how I'm meant to respond has been hugely impactful. So now, whether I am making a big decision related to my business or my personal life, I connect with my Sacral and listen to its response. My Sacral knows what's best for me and my business, which creates so much more freedom and flexibility. It's also allowed me to regain trust in myself and the Universe. My faith in the Universe and my trust in my intuition helps me move past my perfectionist fear of making a mistake. In the past, I would get lost in my head, weighing out all the pros and cons, and then get stuck in indecision.

The only undefined centers I have are my Solar Plexus and my Head Center. With a defined Ajna, I love a mental challenge. I love being in dynamic, engaging discussions with people trying to figure things out. However, I also know I don't need to have all the answers. The inspiration that drops in are possibilities, and I can rely on a more profound understanding that comes from somewhere outside me. This faith and trust in myself and the Divine have helped me overcome my fears and self-limiting beliefs, so I can live out my purpose more fully and unapologetically. Before, I used to be uncomfortable in my skin and had difficulty speaking my truth because I wanted to avoid confrontation. I am now able to be myself authentically. And at the end of the day, isn't that what our purpose truly is? To just be ourselves…? What a wonderful gift Human Design is to us all.

If you're just getting started with Human Design, I recommend first learning about your Type, Strategy, Authority, and Profile Lines as they facilitate a deeper understanding of the roles we're here to play. My Human Design has given me permission to be myself.

I am a 2/4 Profile and I had always struggled with being a weird kind of introvert-extrovert. It depended on my mood or who I was around, as to whether I felt like socializing or keeping to myself. It was freeing to learn that I do need a lot of alone time (I have seven 2nd Lines in my chart!) to feel like myself and that I didn't have to feel guilty about it. Given that I was a people pleaser and also a 4th Line, I would often commit to plans in advance and then on the day of, if I was feeling more introverted, I would have to force myself to muster the energy and head out the door, which was draining. On the days when I was leaning more into my 4th Line energy, if I had to adjust plans because of work or another obligation, I would be fraught with the fear of missing out. This dynamic left me feeling like I didn't really know who I was. Was I an introvert or an extrovert and what determined which "personality" would come out to play on a given day? What I learned through Human Design is that I am both, and I get to decide in each moment what feels good in my body.

The other aspect that has been interesting to explore is how my Profile Lines behave in relationships. As a Relationship and Human Design Coach, understanding these dynamics and how our most intimate relationships often trigger our core wounds is an important exploration into understanding ourselves better. For example, I know that my 2nd Line tends to blame others when things go wrong. Alternatively, I previously believed my happiness depended on whether others were happy. Learning to be accountable for my actions and the experiences I created was a huge area of growth that allowed me to step out of victimhood and into empowerment. My 4th Line, on the other hand, either responds lovingly and supportively toward a significant other, or it freezes them out when the trust has been broken or if there is a fear of getting hurt. Learning how to tear down the walls has been a huge shift for me. Since I am naturally very affectionate and caring, the hardening of my heart pulled me away from my authenticity and purpose and created misaligned relationships and opportunities. It prevented me from tapping into my gifts and using them for the good of those I'm here to serve in this lifetime.

When Human Design is used as a self-discovery tool, it is extremely powerful. One thing I love about Human Design is that you don't have to answer a bunch of qualitative questions that may change based on your mood, your conditioned experience, or your interpretation of the questions. All you need is your birth date, time, and place and voila! You have your chart. Then the fun begins as you begin to experiment and explore what it means to you. It becomes a contemplative guide to understanding how you've been living your Design thus far and a pathway for how you can express it in its highest expression going forward. Human Design helped me redefine my definition of success, reclaim my authenticity and identify a purpose that feels deeply meaningful and satisfying. It can do the same for you!

Corissa Stepp

International Bestselling Author, Speaker,
Relationship and Human Design Coach

2/4 Alchemist (Generator)

Corissa is a Relationship and Human Design Coach as well as an author who helps women rediscover their true authenticity so they can deepen the intimacy in their relationships. She is also a recovering people pleaser and perfectionist and helps guide clients through healing their inner self-critic, letting go of the guilt and the tendency to give more than they have. Together with clients, she helps them release thought and behavioral patterns that are holding them back so they can step into a more empowered, authentic, confident, and interdependent version of themselves and ultimately find a meaningful relationship that aligns with their true value and worth. Corissa also hosts the *Stepping into Meaningful Relationships* podcast.

Corissa had always struggled to find a meaningful way to help others. Then, at the age of forty-one, she experienced a spiritual awakening where she was led to the tools that connected her to her life's purpose. She now wishes to share those tools and healing modalities with others so they can find their own purpose and meaning. Corissa believes that when you deeply connect to your purpose, you also achieve a sense of deep fulfillment, stop caring about what others think, and are able to more courageously and authentically connect with others.

Corissa is a mom to two very-active boys who are her pride and joy. When she isn't working, writing, podcasting, or hanging out at an ice rink or baseball field, you can find Corissa hiking, working out, or singing loudly in the kitchen. She has a bachelor's in quantitative finance and financial economics and is a Quantum Human Design Specialist and a Level 2 Quantum Alignment System Practitioner. Corissa is also a Reiki practitioner, a tarot card reader, an intuitive medium, and a former matchmaker.

Corissa loves working with clients one-on-one in her coaching practice and also offers several group coaching programs including Ditch the People Pleaser Bootcamp and Narcissistic Abuse Recovery Support Group. Check out her website for more information:

corissastepp.com

Follow Corissa on Instagram @corissastepp and check out all the ways to connect with her at:

linktr.ee/corissastepp

Breaking Out of Compromise

By Klara Prosova

I always got what I wanted. It was an interesting pattern in my career that I couldn't miss. But I was only allowing myself to want within boundaries I believed I had no choice but to obey.

On the contrary, there were no boundaries or borders whatsoever whenever I picked up a new digital canvas to create art—no expectations, no rules, no timelines. Just me, the power of my imagination, impulse to play, and indulgence in the process of unexpected discovery.

My second-hand iPad was delivered to the door of my Amsterdam apartment on February 10th, 2021. This was an important milestone, even though it started just like any other of my previous experiments—with pure curiosity to explore something new. I loved those images I saw in my head, and I wanted to see them outside of me too. Would I be able to make them real?

As much as I'd experimented with other creative media throughout my life—fabric, clay, metal clay—drawing and illustrating was unlike anything I'd done before. I had no training in illustrating skills whatsoever, nor did I plan to get any. I never followed a cooking recipe. I never completely followed a hiking trail. I didn't intend to follow drawing tutorials. I trained myself on the job. After all, freedom is everything for me. Digital canvas after canvas, I spent time creating, destructing, recreating, and starting over. It didn't work until it did. And in the process, in my own time and my own way, I was developing the skills necessary to create what I loved to see. And while the space for exploration remains infinite, I have proven to myself yet again that my devotion and focus (being totally involved in what I do) turn me into a creative powerhouse.

Somehow, it was much easier to create what I wanted on a digital paper than it was on a larger scale—my life.

I can trace this back to my childhood, where it all began. There was always something in my life that was controlling, limiting, or restricting me. It started with my upbringing. Then it was the school that was supposed to be the foundation for my career. And then it was the work-life setup I created based on everything I'd learned about how to succeed in life, except that this life was not a fit for me. But at that point, it was the only way I knew to bring in material resources. So, just as in my childhood when I could do what I enjoyed only if and after I'd met all expectations and obligations, that same pattern continued in my adulthood. The purpose of my forty-hour workweek was dedicated to meeting obligations and generating resources, and when I was done with what I needed to do, most of my free time (and the majority of those resources) were devoted to meeting the needs that were otherwise not met.

I needed freedom to use my energy—often spontaneous for my creative self-expression—to follow my own muse instead of responding to tasks. I needed to dream and pursue my visions with no pressure and attachment to the final form they would take, or when (or if) they would take form at all.

I didn't need a midlife crisis to realize that the pharmaceutical industry and traditional ways of working weren't for me and weren't what I wanted—ever. My body and a deep inner knowing told me all of this, but I didn't know how to create what I truly wanted: to honor the energy that wants to move me and express itself through me, and to move in the direction it shows me.

Though my vision of the future was so far away from the life I was living, I knew there was a key. I just couldn't find it. And there was no way I would stop searching for it. So, for thirteen years, I looked for that key. And in the meantime, whatever creative project I was immersed in had to be interrupted with the beginning of a new workweek by Monday, 10 AM, and I'd only hoped the spark of creative energy would return on Friday afternoon. Nothing pained me more than the structures that interfered with my process, that forced me to interrupt my flow, that dictated when I could be available to be moved and when I couldn't—the structures of my own creation, made from confusion and conditioning have led to my own struggle and uneasiness in life.

I maintained this setup with willpower and dedication in the belief that my holy grail was on the other side. I told myself that if I could just stick with it and keep going, I'd eventually get there. In the meantime, despite all the strategies and tactics I tried, I was running myself into the ground as I was trying to manage everything—both what I needed to sustain the flow of resources and what creative outlets I needed. The years were passing by, and I was stuck in a loop of trying to make a change; falling, getting up, falling again, getting up again… trying and not succeeding, and the longer it lasted without seeing my hard efforts leading to change and without understanding why I couldn't figure it out, the more I felt trapped and desperate.

⸺◇⸺

When I have a vision, and an opportunity presents itself that is connected to the vision, there is no challenge that will make it feel unworthy to leap into the experience. I come alive and thrive on adventure that originates from exploring new territories, and I will totally give myself to the experience at hand. It doesn't matter if I don't know what will happen and how the experience will unfold, because even though I may not understand what I'm going through at the time, the true value is always revealed in the end. This keeps me open to experiences wherever I go, such as the one on January 4th, 2021, when I had my Human Design chart explained to me for the first time.

Interestingly, I don't recollect a single concrete memory from that reading; it sits in my body as a blurry experience. What I do remember is that those squares, triangles, lines, colors, and numbers were coding information so personal, specific, and surprising to me that it was quite something to process. If you have been already introduced to your Human Design, you likely know what I am talking about.

It is not often that your world turns upside down and around the way mine did after Human Design was introduced to me. It was profound, and I still view that single experience as an important marker between the "before" and "after." My heart was touched by all the newfound insights, but at the same time, I felt sadness because it reaffirmed how far the very life I had created was from the life I longed to live.

Although my chart suggested that I was essentially born to conquer the art of initiation and creation, the reality was that I'd become the Master of Pharmacy. Although I was born with gifts that yearned to be expressed, that kept seeking their way to the surface and make me come fully alive, I spent about two decades studying and crafting a career that required me to push in a different direction, killing a part of that vitality. That was just how I learned to do life.

My chart validated me, but it didn't give me the key I was seeking. I only felt the gap between the world I had created and the one I dreamed about getting broader, and I didn't know how to create a bridge between the old and the new.

It was too heavy. All those years prior culminated to this point, and I needed a break. So, I paused. And in that pause, my number one priority became slowing down, creating spaciousness and self-care. This is when I ordered my iPad and totally immersed myself in illustrating.

Even though I was purely playing while bringing something new to life, making it visible and experienceable, I was nurturing myself, bringing myself to such a blissful flow with my creation and to my attunement with the present moment. I knew that I was missing nothing. And not only me, but the people I was inviting into my illustrations enjoyed them too. From time to time, I was also publishing reflections from my process and assisting people with creating videos. And I noticed something very interesting about how others were responding.

They found my illustrations playful, igniting curiosity, and triggering reflections and thoughts. They remarked that they were inspired by my journey to dare to do something different, to become immersed in my passion. Those with whom I co-created videos felt comfortable, able to relax into being natural, and to deliver their true selves. They noticed how we co-created without tension and with complete freedom. They appreciated the way I understood the logistics and the linear side of moving things forward while still playing deeply with the magic of the unknown in the creative process. They felt empowered to turn up their light, step through their own fears, and move toward what they wanted to create in their lives.

But the profundity for me in what they were saying was far beyond praise. They were recognizing moments of magnificence I felt in my body. They recognized when I became completely absorbed in the moment and loved every bit of my experience. I barely noticed I was doing any work because it was unlike anything I had known about what it feels like to work, and yet it was bringing such a beautiful impact to their lives. I was. And I wasn't working hard at all to achieve it. My experience was about ease, pleasure, and aliveness. Just like I've always wanted.

And even that isn't all. These people's feedback was pointing at some of the gifts that my Human Design chart was revealing during my contemplation and that I was expressing naturally from my place of inner relaxedness and openheartedness.

To someone who learns that hard work and challenge (to the point of struggle) is what work is about and believes they must do something other than relax into being themselves, this can be a huge, even life-changing revelation.

Over time, it became evident that what started as an unexpected encounter with some chart that was supposed to know me inside and out based on my birth data, turned into a life-changing experience that took me to a whole new encounter with life.

Is it possible that I just discovered my long-desired key?

———◆———

We don't need to know Human Design to live our Design. We already live our Design because it's our imprint. The question is in how we live it.

Up until that point, living my Design had been, in a lot of ways, an uneasy and uncomfortable experience. Even though I got plugged into a lot of good things too, the compromising parts were setting the tone for my overall experience. I had been using my energy to work in a way that meant I must constantly push against my natural drivers and energy pulses while sidelining my needs and desires to express my creativity, which I now know to be fundamental to my well-being. Even though some people would consider my career/job title a great professional achievement and opportunity, I didn't have that feeling because it wasn't what I truly wanted to do, and it required a great deal of inner compromise. In fact, it was making me feel progressively worse, with an impact extending to all areas of my life, including my health and my relationships. I unknowingly taught my body that the struggle, tension, and uneasiness related to this process were normal and necessary, so it took me a while to see value in what I do when I don't feel like I am working.

Although I had a specific role and gifts at my disposal to fulfill that role literally coded in me, I was only occasionally getting a taste of that experience. I was aware of how profoundly different the experiences were on those occasions, but I didn't know what I needed to do to put the desirable experiences at the center of what I was supposed to create. It was as if I had this huge creative capacity (that I felt!) but didn't know how to make the right use of it to reach the kind of success I desired. Every time I tried, it didn't work.

But now with Human Design and Gene Keys (developed by Richard Rudd) illuminating those challenging dynamics, pointing to the imbalance, and giving me clues on how to create alignment, I began to observe with more clarity what was going on without drowning in it, and I also knew what to do and where to channel my energy.

Creating art became the experiment that I eventually began to expand to a larger scale—the creation of my life. I began to consciously collect new experiences as data, noticing where the overlap happened between what I was doing, what I was experiencing, and how it impacted people. I was integrating all the new insights, feelings, and experiences, and anchoring myself in a state of inner connectedness and attunement to my own body's wisdom and truth—and, importantly, acting from that truth. I became more relaxed and excited because the path forward was finally clear. My sovereignty was rising. The self-assuredness I felt was rising. Though I still had a lot of inner work to do, I was literally awakening a new quality of being that began to transform my world from within.

It's freeing to know what you are here to do and what you are not here to do. And unless you are trying to hold on to the known and familiar out of fear of losing something or leaving it behind—whether it's a relationship or a career status, fear of what awaits you in the unknown, or that it will be too hard despite recognizing that it doesn't belong to the life you desire to create and live—it will naturally fall off and make space for the new. In fact, holding on to the old with new awareness becomes highly uncomfortable; once you see it, you'll be pushed from inside to make that revolution. And as soon as you shift your attention and focus and both your mind and body are on the same page, you begin to recreate your reality.

I was not only immensely curious about what beauty I was capable of creating if I had my whole heart in it, but also, I was one hundred percent committed to changing how things were up until this point and doing all the inner work necessary to expand into the full expression of all that I am. But I couldn't put my life on hold. Until my dream could turn into reality in its own time, I needed to maintain the flow of resources while also creating the right conditions for my big creation to take place.

Clearly standing at the beginning of something new, it was my opportunity to decide and define how it was supposed to look moving forward. I was walking in an unknown territory and didn't know if my approach would work, but I knew that if I wanted to create something different from what I had been creating so far, I had to approach this creation unlike anything I have known.

I didn't know how much time it would take for me to make a visible change in my outer life and I didn't want to pollute the realm of my passion by creating from the sense of desperation, lack, and urgency. It was important to me to maintain space for rest and reflection. The point was to recalibrate into my own energy, to examine and free myself from what was buried within me that had been holding me down, and to transform the hidden, unconscious material preventing me from breaking out of the compromise. I placed my focus on developing a whole new skillset, which would allow my inner revolutionary to continue to make gradual shifts and changes within the limitations of my current life. I also found a way to remain in a state of inner relaxedness and continuously be able to separate myself from some of the old foundations, while I was creating what would be solid enough to carry my steps forward.

Possibilities are endless, and it is we who open up to them or stay closed off from them; it is we who pick which ones we will be anchoring into our reality through our every breath and every move. We do it all the time, consciously or unconsciously, so we better do it with awareness and be selective, focus on and nurture what we truly want, and surrender to whatever will get us there.

When we are not clear on what we want and don't want, what we like and don't like, or we don't believe that we can have what we want and like, we don't hold and nurture the vision for what we want to bring into existence, we will compromise and settle for whatever is available or offered to us, dreaming about what we wish we had instead, and perhaps envy those who have it. And when we do that, we settle for a state of dullness, a state that is less than what is possible. In my case, all the experiences in my life prior to this shift were informing this process of selectivity, recognizing what I didn't want moving forward, and focusing on what I wanted more of.

If the life I wanted to leave behind was perpetuating an experience I didn't like, I wondered what if I lay my desired experience as one of my new foundations, and let the creation happen from there? What if I don't dream about it as the goal that happens, and after I do all that I have to do? Which, frankly, has never worked. What if I create the experience I desire now, so that it's always a prerequisite that is met? And whenever I notice that I need to compromise it, I will know it isn't the right step for me and peacefully move away from it.

And in this creative process, I began translating who I am into what I do as a way of making my job an extension of me where vitality, aliveness, and the full and high expression of my nature is the foundation for what and how I create in the world. It is where I can be at my best without inner compromise, so that no matter what I choose to do, I have the full freedom to be myself, to marinate in my own distinct flavor, let it move freely into the world, through the right medium, and touching the right people.

———◆◇◆———

This exploration and learning may never end. But as I continue, it turns out that a big part of my curriculum is to be wise about uncompromised use of my energy, and in that sense, I've gotten great opportunities from which to draw this wisdom. It also turns out that the things I was longing for are deeply in alignment with who I am and how my energy wants to flow when I don't push against it or try to squeeze into a box with parameters that don't fit me. All those feelings of aliveness and expansion, as well as unease and suffering on the more difficult side of the spectrum, were my signals and nudges, showing me the way to what and how I am supposed to be and do. It was my body unconsciously demanding and attempting to live out what it needed—what I needed.

Until this day, I have been playing with multiple outlets and ways for this exploratory and playful creative energy. It hasn't been fixated on illustrating my entire life because there is a broader inclination that then makes me pick the format and medium that fits the expression. So, it's less about what I specifically do and more about how I am involved with what I do. It's about the essence that seeks expression and form and that only needs me to cooperate as it's driven by a curiosity for exploring new possibilities and new feelings through playing at the cusp of the boundaries of what exists.

Yes, there have been events and situations that have obstructed the flow of this energy, but it wasn't even them to blame. Transcending the limitations, rules, boundaries, and boxes (which only compound the misery), unblocking that flow while turning my attention to a more expansive spectrum, holding the intention and anticipation that lifts my spirit, with this deep curiosity for what awaits me there, was up to me.

I am the key. I hold within me the power of change. Human Design and Gene Keys helped me see what to pay attention to; the rest was up to me to get in tune with my body and awareness, to stand up tall and strong for the truth I arrived at, and to find a way to make the necessary changes so that I could have what I want within and without. I mean, what I truly want. At this point, I have no doubt that I have all I need to continue to bring it into existence everyday through my every word and every move, and I am so excited to participate in this unfolding now that I hold a different template for what I want.

Whatever was until now…

What is the next thing you want to create in your life?

If you are like me, you are curious to see what you are capable of creating when you do what you love and love what you do.

When you translate who you are into what you do as a way of moving to a place where your job is an extension of you.

You want to see what is possible when you are free to follow the impulse behind your dream and allow it to become action. Let the dream emerge into the world in a way that is utterly unique and strikingly beautiful, simply because it is your essence seeking expression and form.

And it's not just about art and illustrating.

It's about all of what you call life.

Klara Prosova

Artist, Lifelong Creative, Beauty Translator

4/6 Initiator (Manifestor)

Klara Prosova embodies the impulse to spark new beginnings. She is an artist and lifelong creative, allowing the movement of inspiration, emotion, and imagination to birth newness into existence, both by herself and through co-creation with others.

After a thirteen-year career in the clinical trial industry, Klara decided to combine everything she had learned during her personal, professional, and creative endeavors and step into a new era. Fueled by her passion and a sense of mission, Klara continues to deepen her ability to support herself and others in unlocking the full authentic empowered expression of our nature as a path towards. creating a high-quality experience of life. She strives to rebirth the relationship we have with ourselves so that we can break out of compromise and make our gifts and dreams visible to the world.

Klara's realm of magic lies both within and beyond the five senses. She was born a voracious explorer with an appreciation for the colors and the richness of life and her favorite place in the world is everywhere she can feed her eyes, her ears, and her consciousness with this beauty of diversity.

Klara encourages readers to unapologetically follow the impulse to engage with what makes them come alive and allow it to become action as a way of connecting with the essence of their right work in the world. All her creative work stems from, activates, and supports these impulses and expands the realm of what we believe is possible for us to create in our lives.

Support yourself on your own journey by immersing yourself in her work at:

klaraprosova.com

Follow Klara on Instagram @Klara_Prosova

Reclaiming Yourself

By Jes Francis

There I was being wheeled out on a gurney through cosmetology school and front salon, filled with classmates and clients. This wasn't the first time I had been taken to the emergency room, feeling like I was having some combination of a heart attack and a stroke. I alternated from thinking I might die from the physical symptoms I was experiencing to thinking I would die from embarrassment if it was nothing serious. But one thought was stronger than the rest—I had to be safe because my kids needed me.

A few years prior to this, I had gotten out of two back-to-back unhealthy marriages, to put it mildly. I did what I'd always done. I pulled myself together, put on a brave face, and did what I needed to do to survive and take care of my family. I forgot one vital aspect—taking care of myself. Well, I didn't actually forget. I never really learned in the first place. And when I tried, I was told or made to feel that I was being selfish. That dirty word, selfish.

I could say what led me to my breaking point was all related to unresolved trauma from the two unhealthy marriages, but the truth is it started much earlier in life. From my earliest childhood memories, I felt like an outsider. I spent most of my life masking, conforming, trying to get through, alternating self-isolation with socially induced isolation. I was raised and conditioned to be a good girl, to take care of others, to keep my mouth shut, to be polite and low maintenance, and to pretend everything is okay. The lenses through which I saw the world were gunked up with trauma, patriarchal conditioning, Southern etiquette, Christianity, and all that goes along with being raised around people with addiction. This doesn't mean I wasn't loved and there weren't good times. It's just that these things all colored the way I saw myself, the world, and my place in it in profound ways.

There were so many mixed messages about what was expected of me as a female, what roles, behavior, and characteristics were acceptable. I found myself switching between which parts of myself were safe to be and share within different family or social circles. I'd remind myself to mind my ladylike etiquette here, don't be queer around the Christians, dial down your weirdness, be low maintenance, etc. I'm not good at pretending, so this was exhausting. It was usually easier to just be quiet, to keep things and myself to myself. One thing was clear: Women are meant to put everyone before themselves and take care of self and others without taking any credit.

So, when I broke free from the toxic second marriage, I had the courage and conviction to not repeat that pattern. What I didn't realize is it would require clearing all that gunk off my glasses so I could finally see clearly. I changed my circumstances but continued the pattern of just picking myself up and staying strong for my family—in this case, my kids. I just needed to be their rock and everything else would be okay, right? I did my best to get them the support they needed. As for me, I was convinced that I was fine. I just needed to model a healthy relationship for them and find the right job to make more money while still being home with them. My ADHD, hyperfocus, and poor boundaries were all over these two all-important tasks.

I started to notice I was not tending to my own needs for healing or self-care. I did not even see that as a need. I was the strongest person my friends knew, after all. In reality, I was surviving on sheer willpower, booze, and Mama Bear energy. I was consumed by doing divorce damage control, managing a family and household by myself, taking care of a kid with special needs, and trying to create a better life for my kids. I had a vision of a better life, but I had lost my trust in the Universe and myself for support. I pushed my way through all the adulting and parenting. Then I drank to dull the pain, anxiety, and fear. I thought I had it, that I could handle it. I totally had it. I so didn't have it at all. But it managed to get me through a few years.

After the embarrassingly public panic attack alarm at cosmetology school, I knew something had to change. I had finally pushed myself too hard, too far, ignored myself too long. I had no choice. I had to make some changes to keep those panic attacks from recurring; I had to remove some energy leaks from my life. It was time to clean house, literally and metaphorically.

I left a relationship that was no longer right for me. I quit smoking and drinking. Drinking and smoking had not always been a problem for me. But, over the past couple of years, I formed an unhealthy dependence on them to numb my feelings of anxiety, fear, self-doubt, and dissonance with my life. It helped me ignore my wants, needs, and feelings that felt too overwhelming, out of reach, or invalid. I really thought this tactic was helping me be more functional. It took multiple panic attacks and health scares to make me realize that I actually just needed better tools for coping with this human existence. I dove into self-development. I learned how to clean up my thinking and started to remember what really mattered to me.

After making those few lifestyle changes, I really thought my self-care work was resolved. I moved on to focus on finding that perfect career to support my family, one I actually found meaningful and fulfilling at the same time. I was convinced finding this perfect career was going to solve all my remaining issues. Well, I did find my dream job! And what I leaned eventually through my training is that the solution to that meaning and fulfillment and good life I was trying to provide wasn't through the perfect career, it was through finding and embracing my true self again.

When you're living out of alignment, you may notice it manifesting as:

- mental exhaustion
- physical burnout
- numbing out with alcohol, food, TV, or overwork
- people-pleasing at your own expense
- feeling like a shell of yourself
- hitting your limit of tolerating
- blow ups or breakdowns
- increased stress, anxiety, maybe even panic attacks
- new or chronic health issues
- headaches
- fatigue
- feeling stuck frustrated, resentful, or bitter

Maybe you've hit your limit, and you know something's gotta give. Something has to change. You want more from your life. More meaning, more fulfillment, more joy, and more satisfaction, but how the heck do you get there? Especially when you're already exhausted. Maybe you're feeling super overwhelmed. You might've already tried a bunch of these things, a bunch of things that didn't stick or work.

What I know now is that you must align to and embrace your true self before your purpose can unfold in your life. If you don't really know yourself, you're probably living out someone else's values and purposes. If you don't value yourself, you will not give yourself the care and attention you need. If you don't trust yourself, you probably aren't making the most aligned choices and decisions.

I'd like to share with you three things I wish I'd known sooner to aid you in creating these shifts for yourself.

- The myths of selfishness
- Willpower is not enough
- It is all a practice

Knowing, valuing, and trusting yourself is not *selfish*. Have you ever been called selfish or been afraid of being accused of being selfish? When you hear the word selfish, how does it feel in your body? I think most of us have experienced selfish as a bad or dirty word. I know I have.

The definition of *selfish* is caring only about what you want or need without any thought for the needs or wishes of other people.

The problem with this definition is when the word *selfish* is used to shame people who are just trying to care for and be true to themselves. And that is not selfish. The more you tend to knowing yourself—truly knowing your strengths, needs, and what's important to you— the better you're able to communicate when you can show up as your authentic self. It enriches all areas of your life when you know yourself well enough to know how to best support yourself and others. How can that be selfish? And, if it's not selfish, what is it?

Let's explore the antonyms of *selfish*. We have self-forgetful, selfless, and self-sacrificing. *Oof.* Neither of these extremes—selfish or selfless seem to be very helpful to me. You? I mean if you are reading this book, you are at least curious about living a life full of purpose and meaning. I guess the question is, are you going to live by someone else's purpose and meaning or your own? I invite you to let that sink in.

Forgetting myself, being less than my true self, and self-sacrifice are what led me to my mental and physical limits and breaking down. We aren't made to be anyone but ourselves. That is not selfish. That is being. It just is. We come into this life with a body, mind, and spirit. If we deny it, neglect it, try to morph it into something else, what do we expect to happen?

Think of a car for a moment. And this car is your transportation to all the things you need in life—food, work, visiting loved ones. If you don't care for this car, by putting in the proper gas for your make and model, by practicing care for your car, providing oil and fluid changes, by using parts that are made for that make and model, by being mindful of the terrain you're traveling on, what will happen? Your car isn't being selfish by needing regular unleaded instead of EV88 or by having to work hills a little differently because it's a front-wheel drive versus a four-wheel drive. It just needs what it needs to perform at its best. Its abilities and best performance look different than other models and other cars. You get the picture. Being who you are, taking the time to know and care for yourself in your unique ways, and following your own path is not selfish. It is self-full. It is self-nourishing. It is being true to you. It is necessary.

When I was trying to be selfless, I didn't do my best at meeting others 'needs or my own. My childhood generational and societal conditioning really set me up to believe the story that I was supposed to put taking care of everyone else first *and* be fulfilled by that. Of course, like many, I had conflicting messaging to be a strong, independent woman at the same time as being selfless and nurturing and attractive—and not too loud.

As you set forth to know, value, and trust yourself in new ways, don't fall into the trap of relying on willpower alone to create these new habits and beliefs.

Willpower alone is not enough. It will never be enough to help you reach your goals. It'll never be enough to carry you through continual self-sacrificing. It will never be enough to push through burnout. Our minds are made up of conscious processes and unconscious processes. The unconscious processes take up about 95 percent of your mind power. The conscious processes make up the remaining 5 percent. Willpower exists as a conscious process. So, even if you're in the minority of people who have a defined Will Center and have more consistent access to will, it is still only 10 percent of your mind power. You have 90 percent of your mind repeating subconscious scripts and conditioning. We each also have our own unique mix of traumas, genetics, energy levels, etc. Willpower can be temporarily helpful and life serving—*saving* at times—but it can't fuel you alone.

You can't "willpower," push, or think your way out of limiting beliefs, generational trauma, or automatic subconscious scripts that are running your behaviors. This requires a more holistic approach of identifying your limiting beliefs, programming, and conditioning, releasing them from your body and subconscious, and finally creating new empowering and aligned beliefs.

Willpower is like wanting so hard you push something into existence. You can use that wanting to fuel your actions and behavior changes. It can be very powerful. But when your energy is low or other challenges arise, you're likely to slip back into old, misaligned habits and patterns, because this is the path of least resistance. Willpower is not as effective when your energy resources are low.

Living in our modern world gifting us with so many demands, challenges, distractions, and responsibilities, it is even more helpful to have a backup for willpower. That backup is all about subconscious programming. Clearing outdated, unhelpful limiting subconscious programming and replacing it with new stories and programming that align with your current goals, values, and desires will support you when your energy is lower. It will help you stay on track and in alignment when the demands of life are high and you're too tired to rely on your conscious effort.

Before I learned to create and practice new stories for myself, I turned to unhealthy habits and relationships when I was overthinking, exhausted, or anxious. After giving my subconscious new optimal stories and replacement behaviors, it has become much easier to stay in alignment than when I was trying to fuel these thought and lifestyle changes on willpower alone.

You might be feeling overwhelmed or drained at this point and that's understandable. I want you to know that it gets better. Giving yourself the attention and nurturing you need won't prevent challenges from showing up in your life, but you'll likely feel more stable through the challenges. As you come into alignment, you may notice your emotional baseline becoming more peaceful or calm. The more you care for yourself, the easier it is to return to that peaceful state of being.

Life is all a practice. It's a practice of healing, of gaining awareness, of deconditioning, of showing up and interacting with the world in an authentic way. The definition of practice is the actual application or use of an idea, belief, or method as opposed to theories relating to it. Knowing yourself is a practice. Trusting yourself is a practice. Loving yourself is a practice. Being in alignment with your mind, body, and spirit is a practice.

Now, the ongoing practice of getting to know, value, and trust yourself, creates alignment with your true authentic self, and then you won't have to try so hard. This is where the real magic happens, and your purpose unfolds naturally. You'll start to notice synchronicities and things happening for you that match your authentic true self. Things you saw in your chart that excited you are now happening and are showing up in your world presenting as signs, connections, and invitations. This is what happens when you give yourself the gift of healing and alignment and when you give yourself the gift of your own attention and tending.

I want you to know you're allowed to be your authentic self. And that is exactly what the world needs. It is where the magic is. It is what is best for your loved ones whether they know it or not. Loving and nurturing your true self is a gift to everyone around you and creates a ripple effect. It can be hard to believe that taking time for yourself is not actually taking away from others. It can be hard to believe that expressing your truth is for the higher good. It is true even when people around you want you or expect you to be a different way or to stay the same as you once were. But as you go through the process of aligning to your authentic self, the disruptions and responses are just a blip compared to the synchronicities and increasing moments of joy, delight, and inner peace. You will start to notice a sense of calm becoming your baseline as you trust your intuition, your Strategy and Authority, and your right timing. You might not even be the first person to notice these changes.

My youngest daughter noticed and started pointing out how much calmer I was in stressful situations. She noticed how much calmer and in flow my driving had become. Of course, I'm still human and I have my moments or hours or even days of feeling grumpy or falling back into reactionary behaviors. And this is completely natural as we build new habits, new neural pathways, and new stories about ourselves. But when you allow yourself to know, love, and trust yourself, everything else gets easier. It's strange to say that and really believe it. It's not that nothing bad ever happens to you or in your life, or that there's never a struggle or negative feeling. That's all still there. What changes is your experience of those human feelings and circumstances. You don't have to be miserable, a shell of yourself just surviving the rest of your life. The struggle and discomfort of transformation, of coming home to yourself, is completely worth it.

I came to my life purpose through training to help others live an all-around healthy and fulfilling life. Health coach school taught me all about the ingredients to nourishing the mind, body, and spirit, but not how to create change in a sustainable and lasting way. Hypnotherapy school taught me how to access the subconscious mind to align unconscious programming with conscious desires and goals. Learning Human Design brought it all together for me. It gives a blueprint and context for the human experience.

I learned how to make aligned decisions that I can trust through my Human Design Type, Strategy, and Authority. The more I practice following my Type, Strategy, and Authority, the deeper my trust with myself and Source/Spirit/the Universe grows.

Learning to see the Human Design chart as a catalog of archetypes, each with a gift and purpose, really helped me start to value myself like never before.

Human Design has helped me personally align with my purpose by shining a light on what was and has always been there within me—the parts of me that I took for granted, discounted, or dismissed because they are so familiar to me. And now with more awareness, I can expand to a higher expression of what's always been a part of me. I get to explore all the ways I can lean into my consistent energies to carry and spread more love and joy and have more adventures. I just really appreciate myself and what I've got more of now. It makes life more fun! I get to explore the wisdom and fluidity of my open centers. When I'm feeling scattered or lacking direction, I can look to my chart for guidance on where to direct my energies in a purposeful way. I was already on a healing and helping path and Human Design gave me a massive up-level of understanding. It is truly a brilliantly accurate framework for understanding and growth.

Jes Francis

Author, Holistic Coach, Hypnotherapist, and
Human Design Guide

4/6 Alchemist (Emotional Generator)

Jes Francis was born and raised in Little Rock, AR. She currently resides in Louisville, KY, and enjoys connecting and working with people all over the world virtually. Purpose by Human Design is her debut as a published author. Jes loves to coach, teach, and write about all things self-love, self-care, and life purpose.

Jes is a heart centered, queer feminist on a mission to support others who have ever felt like outsiders or misfits. She achieves this through guiding those who feel lost or overlooked to reclaim themselves, their vitality, and purpose. She believes Human Design can be a fun and empowering tool for healing, self-awareness, and expansion. It is her deepest desire to aid in the healing of people and the planet, creating sustainability for all, together.

Jes is the mother to three super awesome humans, a dog, and a cat. Jes is a former licensed massage therapist now certified in Quantum Human Design and Quantum Alignment Systems by Karen Curry Parker, Traditional Human Design, Integrative

Nutrition health coaching, NLP (neuro linguistic programming), and hypnotherapy. She is currently working on a degree in mind-body psychology.

Jes encourages readers to give themselves permission to go on this journey of self-reclamation. She invites you to explore your Human Design further with a reading or to be supported on a deeper level through one of her 1:1 programs. Learn more at:

JesFrancis.com

Follow Jes on Instagram @jes_francis

The Empowered Heart:
How Human Design Helped Me Out of
Victim Consciousness

By Sharon Schneider

Victim Consciousness

The beautiful antique sash windows with their grand appeal seem menacing now in these long early hours of the morning. The icy, gale-force winter wind creeps in the room. The heat from the charming fireplace has long since escaped, and now all that's left is the darkness, the cold wind, and me. I have my bed partner within arm's length, but I feel completely alone.

I chose this quaint old dame as our home-away-mine;from-home in the winter months this year. I chose for us to be here. I couldn't stand the thought of another grueling audit deadline season alone, this time with Sebastian, our now two-year-old, and another baby on the way. *Being alone with my toddler and my unborn baby might be okay,* I think, *if it wasn't for the fear that has found its home under my skin, since our toddler's got his wriggle on and is moving around unassisted.* Without any rational explanation, I've become paranoid and am living in constant fear that he may drown.

It's not easy in my skin.

I've hustled for us to tag along on this work trip. Cape Town is the new and exciting hometown on the horizon in our family's future. We'll be moving here permanently, soon. The exact details are shaky again. We had a date, then it was postponed by the corporate machine powers that be. I can't stand the on-again off-again uncertainty, so I figure this trip was the perfect opportunity for me to help things along a bit. And it's the perfect excuse to not be left back in the old.

I'm restless. I can't be left behind this time. Change is coming, I can taste it. So during the long hours of Paul's, my preoccupied husband, workday, I'll be scouting for houses and schools and finding general answers to questions that come with relocating and the important work of raising a family.

But, instead of feeling enlivened—being here, in this new and exciting space—something feels off.

Very much off. The sick feeling in my gut won't let me rest.

I'm fighting back panic, my arms around my belly.

The same questions swirling in my head. *When last did I feel him kick? How can I not remember something so important?*

There's been some drama since we arrived. A comedy of errors of sorts. My mind's a muddle. We've backed the rental car into a wall down the long narrow driveway.

We're tense and fighting all the time. In fact, no, there's not a lot of time together, just a few stolen moments for fighting after long hours of high-pressure work for Paul, all the way across town. For me, the hard work is here. Being in my skin. The work of being a mom to our toddler and a grumpy pregnant mom at that. Long hours alone here in the house, my tummy, this fear, our two-year-old, and me.

And there's the business of these antique doors. Who knew? Knee-high doorknobs, which have proven perfectly accessible for our toddler trying out his new skill of turning keys, causing more chaos. Last night, it meant me locked in the loo, and our toddler locked out, in this strange house complete with an open wood fire burning. The cherry on top, the uniquely South African occurrence of load shedding, which is basically, suburb-wide, prearranged black outs. Power outages, on a rotation schedule. As our bad luck would have it, load shedding at the exact wrong time—nightfall, with me locked in the loo, and with a petrified toddler in the house.

So, there's been some stress.

My head is full, confused, and preoccupied. But surely, I can find that important information in my brain. Was it days ago? Hours? When can I actually remember the sensation of a kick?

Is this all in my head? I'm just a normal, albeit paranoid, expectant mother, surely?

Maybe he's just sleeping in there…or making his way out, perhaps?

Grasping and groping my tummy, I wish the little man inside could speak, and assure me he's okay. I try to convince myself he's coming early. I'm sure of it.

Could today be the day?

I poke and prod.

Nothing.

My very round, 33-week pregnant tummy gives me no response.

The lack of sleep is a struggle I'm not accustomed to. Waiting is the very opposite to what I do.

I hustle.

I strive.

I fix.

Ironically, lying here in the dark, there's nothing I can do but wait.

I have no answers.

Answers will come many hours later after I have convinced myself forward into action. Convincing Paul is also apparently important in order to mobilize myself. His best advice is that I'm being paranoid, but it won't harm to get a doctor to give me a checkup. So, while chugging down a coffee and a chocolate bar in the hopes of getting my baby moving—to feel something—I hurry to find an obstetrician in a strange town, an apparently impossible task. Sufficiently panicked, finally I realize the only way is straight to the closest hospital and getting my tummy hooked up to a heart rate monitor in the emergency room. I'm not quite sure why it takes me so long to find this direct line of action to some peace of mind, if nothing else. I call Paul, who went off to deal with his day. Now he knows, from my tone, something is definitely wrong. By the time he arrives at the ER, we've established there's no traceable heartbeat.

Then there is immediate and close attention from a doctor. Baby's heart may be undetectable because my pelvis bone could be in the way. We need a full scan. There's a chance he's okay.

Initiation

Swiping up and down and left to right with the cold jelly over my hump, my gaze meets the doctor's and then we both stare into the monitor: I'm hopeful.

Our eyes meet again—hers are sympathetic but confident; mine, desperate. I know. Immediately I can tell our little baby boy is gone. Of course, there is no sound. *There should've been the sound of a beating heart. And there's nothing moving on the screen.* She points to the monitor: the chambers, the valve within the heart—silent, stillness, black. On one level I just don't understand. *How can this be happening?* I didn't even know babies died this late into pregnancy. This is not a miscarriage. I know about miscarriages. We've miscarried before. But this? I didn't anticipate this. I thought we were in the clear now. He could easily survive if he was born today.

My human brain takes a while to play catch up with a deep sense of knowing within my soul.

I know this story. It's racing up to the foreground to meet me.

This moment of life-changing adversity brings with it a richness of emotional experience. So many different feels all at once. All the usual suspects.

Shock, devastation, disbelief, disappointment, sadness. So. Much. Grief.

So much to process and yet each emotion is brilliant, complex, and clear. Along with these, there's something else. Unexpected. Positive. It's the feeling of relief. Immediate, complete, undeniable. The fear feeling is gone—the preoccupation with drowning. For a year or more, the sick-with-worry feeling is completely and magically gone.

It's the dreadful, bittersweet answer to my prayers.

There's more.

More sweetness. An abundance of blessings. A feeling I can't explain.

What on Earth does this mean?

My mind knows better than to fight something that feels good in a moment where life is bending down so low.

There's an opening for faith and *I choose that*.

The life and death of my baby boy will have great purpose. I will make this life lesson count. A *knowingness* that good comes from this.

Within the week, I journey away from being an eternally immature child, to new shores. Finally, I'm now an alumnus. A graduate from the school of struggle.

I go from being almost entirely externally referenced and preoccupied with the opinions and happiness of others to something new—an awareness of myself. My own Truth, on my own terms.

It feels like an invitation into something full and complete and sweet.

The exploration will bear fruit almost a decade down the line with more reinforcement from each day I'm challenged with the task of asserting myself, with standing in my power, having my voice heard as I'm once again surrounded by a family of powerful voices. I'll get to review this lesson daily in the school of parenting, in a way that's reminiscent of my home growing up, also the odd one out amongst vocal powerhouses. Only now, I'm an adult with life experience and the foundational alchemizing ingredient of a growing understanding of my own Human Design, and the understanding of theirs.

I will lay a foundation in the years to come that will support me as I take the reins more and more and believe in myself and my own capabilities each and every day with my greatest teachers, my two boys. For me, the first and most important lesson within my Human Design journey is understanding who I am *not*. The openness in my chart combined with my own unique soul curriculum has had me in a chaotic tangle of over-giving, over-loving, and codependency combined with biting off more than I can chew, leaping without a safety net; an overwhelming combination that has had me searching for answers, sometimes in emptiness. I recall those cold dark places like drugs and alcohol in my twenties to more elegant and awake solutions like meditation and breath work in my thirties, and eventually, as I ramp up the stakes with more complicated family and relationship dynamics, the understanding of human beings through Human Design in my forties. *This* will be the invaluable magic mix to getting me on my feet and keeping me there.

First, the long kilometers home through the night, under the lonely light of a waxing moon.

Tomorrow, our own hometown, our own people, our own doctor.

Precious days follow for my soul's motives to be made clear through surreal messages from Spirit and heaven-sent Earth angels in the guise of doctors and nurses, friends and family, divinely assigned to hold me steady and in compassion, as I allow for something powerful to be birthed within the experience of this deep loss.

Our doctor weighs risks and tells us we must deliver naturally. Laboring to bring forth the lifeless body of our baby boy seems like a cruel joke from the Universe. Wrestling in my mind. Resistance in my body. After four days attempting to induce labor, it seems it's not working. My body will not yield and open.

Our Earth angel nurse brings more truth. If the induction doesn't work, the c-section option includes with it recovery time and pain consequences I hadn't considered. *How could I know?*

She explains with a natural delivery, my body's health is instantly restored. No perpetuation of pain through weeks hunched over a cesarean scar with no newborn baby distraction and the accompanying oxytocin-assisted healing that goes with it. She shares with me her experience with her own stillborn baby. Her story of loss is strikingly similar to ours; it's evidently heaven-sent. She knows deeply how we feel. I feel seen by all that is.

Informed Self-Empowered Response

The new information is a catalyst. A turning point. I make a choice and it changes my world. I choose to support myself, to rise up and meet my own needs, something I've been yearning for—an unmet need I was unaware of.

I make the decision to bounce on the labor ward birthing ball as if I have some sort of victory imminent. Hours of non-stop bouncing follow. There's a newness in how I perceive myself and everyone in the world outside of me. *This is my experience.* No one else knows or *could* know. It's all up to me. There is no external opinion or expectation. There's nothing to prove. I can, however, show up for myself in a profound way. With persistence, endurance, and the new perspective, I shift from the victim to being my own hero and grab the hand being offered to me by my soul.

I have an uncanny self-assurance and lightness come over me, and almost miss the sad irony in this natural delivery. Something I wanted to do desperately the first time with Sebastian, but my body wouldn't dilate. It's not the natural delivery I could have anticipated but through the birth canal of struggle, came my own rebirth into empowerment.

A Quantum Leap

This experience jumps me from one train track to the next.

After this experience, I choose to look at the world through fresh, open eyes with the faith and conviction of my own inner knowing.

It's not perfect by any means. There's the continued process of parenting, and my struggle with being under pressure to prove myself, to be seen and heard, to make meaning, and be on purpose—consistent, diligent attention and awareness needed for this.

Thankfully because of the challenge, I have something significant enough in magnitude to shift me completely out from underneath the weight of the conditioning of the old. I catch a glimpse of my true empowered self, as I will come to understand her almost a decade down the track through Human Design—an imprinting of my divine essence.

Staying rock solid and steady in the storm and finding my power there has helped me to spread love and change the world a little.

If there was a way to understand this message from the Universe in another way—without having to go through the trauma of losing a child whereby I simply understand how to shift from reactivity as a result of my own unmet needs, vulnerabilities, and challenges into empowered responsiveness—I would list it all up eloquently and elegantly with Human Design (but living it makes it forever). Here's how the explanation might look.

Reacting: Under Pressure and the Fear of Failure

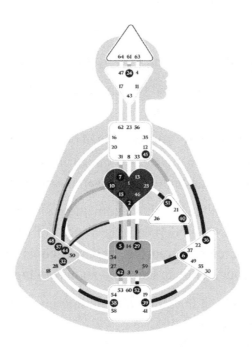

Sharon Schneider's Human Design Chart

What feels most challenging to me in my chart is my undefined Throat and the seeking of attention and recognition that goes with it. It's particularly tough when there is challenging conditioning that has one feeling like the odd one out. My family of origin and my family as it is now, all have powerful definition in their Throat Centers. To me, it feels like the root of my own victim consciousness. There is more though. I'm an Alchemist/Generator, with a whole lot of openness.

Having the undefined Head, Ajna, Throat, Root, and Will Centers means I'm under a lot of problem-solving pressure and pressure to act, in order to make myself visible so that I might prove myself worthy. Added to the pressure to do is the paralyzing opposing force not to do, created from a fear of failure, another theme threading through my chart which adds more tension to the mix.

- The fear gates of the Spleen, of which I have a good majority defined.
- A double dose in the trial and error, failure-sensitive nature of the 6/3 Profile.

- Another couple doses in my Incarnation Cross, that essentially speaks of a need to overcome.

The last of the major victim consciousness threads running through is the theme of over-caring and over-giving that live in the shadow frequencies within my chart.

- My Incarnation Cross and Kiron Gates 10, 15, 6 and 27 flavor my specific reaction response with over-loving, and over-doing.
- Add to that the empathy of the open Emotional Solar Plexus, and I'm just more about reading the needs of those around me than having any idea of what's happening inside.

I know I'm not alone. No matter what our charts look like, we have some challenges to face, to grow through, and to rise above.

If you are open or undefined in certain centers, notice that. Where are you reacting to the energy of others, rather than responding from your own energy? Create a thorough understanding from the inside of how that is impacting you in a way that may be keeping you off course.

Hold close to your heart the part of the story that is who you are and notice carefully what is happening in your world that is purely a result of how you manage people and relationships—where you are absorbing and amplifying the story of others because of openness and variability in your own experience. The insight from Human Design is oftentimes most powerful when kept simple. I've noticed that by focusing on the vulnerabilities to conditioning and sensitivity in the openness of the centers, as well as the general themes threaded through the chart, within the Profile, and the Incarnation Cross, etc. I'm able to work most effectively within the everyday traps of the thoughts and feelings that perpetuate the story of old, in order to create change.

As sensitive people, we are taking people in. We are often driven to serve, to love, and to create change and healing on the planet. And boy, oh boy, that can be one frustrating life agenda when constantly stuck and bogged down, not only in the energy of others but also in the perpetual nosedive downward spiral of over-giving.

Up until this point, my life has been about decisions made under pressure with the unique themes of over-caring and codependency plus my own self-created vortex into victim mode and the creation of chaos. The most eloquent of all the many profound lessons of Human Design for me is understanding and embodying the TRUTH, the actual embodiment within my own energy and not the impact on myself created by what others think, feel, and expect. (Through no fault of anyone else but my own self.)

When parenting my powerhouse children, I'm constantly tested. They are Manifestors, here to initiate and inform, and I'm here to respond. This can become a perpetual cycle of acting under pressure to figure things out for them by over-giving and over-loving, empathizing, and stealing their lessons to prove my own worth and lovability, in order to force my "goodness" onto them and into the world. I make sure to keep them happy and steady, read their energy so I can adapt and morph, keep the peace, please, and avoid the truth—even lie when necessary to keep everyone calm and happy. They are both emotionally defined. There's the trap of getting it wrong enough times to know that of course I cannot *make* them happy. I cannot raise them to feel content and powerfully independent by shielding them, placating them, and running in every direction when they shout out.

The blessing of a life-changing experience such as mine is that I was given the opportunity to focus inwards, once, in a profound way that my body remembers through time. With nowhere to go and no one to fix, there was only me. Taking care of my own true and deep needs for this one magical yet tragic moment in time, and having the moment etched in my brain and body as a significant reference point for years to come was truly a defining moment. (I have, of course, met the superficial needs before—the ones satisfied under social pressures of finding a mate and landing the job that pays well or proves something.) This is a real and important need that I almost overlooked. In that excruciating moment, I chose. I responded. I was seen by the infinitely magical people that surrounded me as well as by Spirit. Now I see myself. I value who I am. With determination, I have created a new outcome: the start of my own transformative understanding.

Empowered Heart

Being nice, being the good person and doing the right thing for everyone else was never going to work. This is codependency. This was me stealing power and life lessons from the people I loved the most.

Fifteen years ago today, I made a big decision at the end of a big all night, all weekend, all decade-long bender to stop the drinking and the non-stop drug dabbling that had pretty much lasted throughout my twenties. Unbeknownst to me, the Universe was plucking me up out of the chaos and placing me very gently on the roof to find a gentle life partner and have some powerhouse children to keep me slightly hypervigilant and on track to finding my own inherent empowerment and learn a bit through people-watching from a distance.

Living with my openness, with the weight of responsibility to meet the needs of everyone, as well as the tension between doing and not doing, and between fear and love, had me entrapped. Parenting along with the wisdom and insight of my chart provides me with the fertile ground for transformation. Every day I get to practice the shift into the high vibrational expressions within my chart because I am a mother working hard in this high-stakes environment of nurturing from a place of unconditional and empowered love. I'm stumbling and fumbling often, but there is always the awareness of what is *not* mine, of what is conditioned, of where I am reacting to them, or perhaps *because* of them. I am aware of where I'm under pressure to please them and to solve their problems, to do for them what they are perfectly capable of doing themselves, of becoming entangled, and then stopping to pause. There is the knowing that there is always the opportunity to reset and start again tomorrow. It feels hard won, but I've found within my own Human Design a powerful story of love in response to the world and people within it. This is what I choose each day, rather than adrenaline, the hypervigilance, the reading of the room, the pressure to fix and do, and the feeling of failure when it's never enough.

I know that when I am clear on my needs separate from theirs, and when I'm clear on their energy separate from my own, the presence within parenting follows (with the added bonus of being present to and loving of myself).

I'm a 6th Line Profile with three very distinct phases to my life, the third of which is yet to come. Things are already looking completely different.

Finally, it seems I'm harvesting the message of Max, my stillborn baby, more than seven-years-old now. There's the shock in the awakening process of my own power, but more than that, there has been a change that has moved everything in the direction of serving my highest and best good as well as the good of everyone around me. There is the emergence of purpose. A victory. A personal transformation from victim consciousness to empowerment, but one that is permeating into all I do.

If I could speak to that girl—the me back then at the time of losing Max—and whisper in her ear of what she had bravely chosen to open up to, I could tell her of the perfection within this creation. Having been touched by the angelic presence, the messages from Spirit, the reassurance of our baby coming back, and the phoenix, as well as the Earth angels that surrounded us in those days in the delivery room, I know that I was there on some level—this me, future me, or perhaps the far greater version of me that is one with all things, my Higher Self. This is what I knew back then. The feeling I felt. The blessings I could sense. *This is it.*

This is a creation of a new world for me and my children, one of empowered tranquility. It has meant not only finding the power within but also finding sufficient daily energy and faith with good decisions around health and well-being as well as the invaluable Human Design roadmap to the truth.

Sharon Schneider

Transformation Agent, Yogi, and Writer

6/3 Alchemist (Generator)

Sharon is an intuitive agent for change. For two decades Sharon's focus has been on creating spiritual health and emotional well-being and has been teaching, coaching, and guiding people for fifteen of those years. Sharon uses empowerment tools and techniques including breath work, yoga, meditation, and more recently, Human Design. She passionately guides powerful people through seemingly insurmountable challenges, returning them to their innate magic.

She lives the knowingness that transformation is possible for everyone who seeks it. She believes in initiating events that often occur; events that make us feel like the world is ending. She sees these moments as being the beginning of a powerful heart-based upgrade for ourselves and for the world we live in.

She is inspired to share how she's been initiated by the experiences of life to create big and lasting change internally, and in the world around her. Her own challenges with self-imposed limiting beliefs and an overburdened autonomic nervous system have created a deep passion within her to guide people to their own empowerment.

She believes in the initiating turning point that life often presents. When pairing this initiation with a profound connection inward through devoted daily practice (i.e., breathwork, meditation, yoga), one has the potential to generate the powerful life force energy necessary to create a breakthrough. And with the added guidance of the Human Design blueprint, we can achieve the shift into a new vision of the fullness of the life we choose.

This is freedom. This is power.

Sharon is a boy mom to her most important teachers. She lives with her man team, including her pillar-of-strength husband and her strong-willed Scottish Terrier, on the Surf Coast near Melbourne, Australia.

Sharon leads When Powerful People Change, a bespoke ten-week transformational program designed to dramatically excavate limiting beliefs and stuck programming, realigning people with their high frequency expression as it is chosen. Her program has been created for readers who are ready to utilize the power within the struggle, the power latent within a turning point, to create a quantum leap into the fullness of their personal strength and potential. Sharon has been described by her clients as a tour de force, and a source of energy.

Follow Sharon on Instagram @sharon_schneider_

Finding Unity Within:
Releasing the Illusion of Separation

By Alana Heim

The stars above me shine brightly. I feel like an insect, drawn to the dazzling lights. I delightfully sigh. As the millions of sparkles dance across the vast sky, I feel comfortable and safe. I drift into oneness with the energy. Love and gratitude fill my heart and mind. I am calm.

My gaze shifts allowing the silhouette of pine trees overhead to bring me down to earth and back to reality. I am nestled in my warm sleeping bag in the back of our diesel truck. The mattress beneath me is soft and supportive. There is a deliciously cool breeze tickling my face. My husband is snoring softly. He and my son are peacefully sleeping on either side of me. The girls are asleep inside the truck. The majestic Mount Shasta in all her glory stands in the darkness behind me fewer than twenty miles away.

All is still. All is quiet. All is well.

The stars are magnificent, I think. *Hmm. Have I ever truly slept under the stars before?* I cannot recall. However, my mind is quick to follow the trail of eventful crumbs that led me to this moment.

I smile realizing the many planned and unplanned events were divinely orchestrated. All because I chose to listen, allow, and act according to what felt aligned and true for me. *And here I am. Seeing myself shine as brilliantly as the cosmos and the stars above.* The purpose for the trip was beyond what I could have anticipated. *Trust and follow my intuition.*

As a Projector, part of my Design and purpose is to trust myself and the higher power of Source that I am seen, loved, and supported. Has this been easy for me? No way! It's something I've been learning and am still fine tuning. To sit under those captivating stars and feel connected as one with the cosmos was only possible because I chose to let myself flow with my right-brain instincts that were guiding me to trust.

The deeper my 1/3 Profile dives into Human Design through investigating and experimenting, the more I rediscover the parts of me that long to be acknowledged, valued, and understood by me. Without an "*inner*standing" of myself, how can I expect others to get me?

In my Human Design chart, I have a Large Split. This is where I need at least two or more gates to bridge the two separate parts in my chart. My Head and Ajna Centers are connected via Channel 64/47. My Will and Emotional Solar Plexus Centers are connected through Channel 37/40.

With a split as part of my Design, it makes sense why I struggle with feeling separated from Source. By my own personal Design, I feel separation within myself. In the past, this separation caused me to doubt myself. My mind would encourage me to *plan* for the how in life rather than *trust* my emotions' ability to guide it to come forth naturally. The confusion in my mind kept me running on a hamster wheel of distrust. The thought of *how will this happen?* enticed me to be the lab animal stuck in a never-ending cycle of chasing answers I believed I had to create.

While my mind raced along in this loop, I disassociated from my body.

"Mom. Mom. Moommm." My kids would repeat my name multiple times. I never heard them. I was light years away. My physical appearance presented as any other human, but mentally I was vacant, distant, and unavailable. This didn't make for being a guiding and loving parent.

"Alana, where are you? We need you to be more present." My supportive Projector husband, Mike, would gently and firmly remind me. Hearing this information would jar me back to reality. It would hurt to hear this. As the feeling of imbalance ripped through me, tears shot down my face. *My family needs me.*

My emotions initiated the tears, and just as quickly, my mind would command them to shut off. This would trigger me mentally. *Right when I'm finally doing well in business, I'm failing my family,* I'd think with irritation. What I soon learned is my emotions were stepping up and growing louder so I'd finally pay attention to them. They had their own version to the story I never allowed myself to *feel*.

This was the other part of me, my defined Will and Emotional Solar Plexus that I avoided like the plague. Through dissociation, my mind wandered off into fairy-tale land, dreaming of what could be or should be. Back on Earth, I ignored my family and my own physical body. Deep within me, the repressed part of myself knew that if I was to fully trust myself, I'd have to operate from my Emotional Authority. It was time for me to connect to my emotions. Not just *think* I'm feeling, but to allow those emotions to have a place in reality.

My Emotional Tribal Wave sought to belong and feel connected in a balanced way of honoring myself and others. With a Piscean Sun sign, it's kind of funny I was unaware that my Design is reflective of truly being the two fish swimming in opposite directions—mainly against myself. It soon became apparent that knowing how to trust myself, and more importantly, *which* part of myself to trust, was something I needed to work on.

It was a challenge to trust, especially when I didn't know who I was through the lens of Human Design. Once I learned to differentiate between the parts of myself that radiate out into the world (defined centers) versus the parts that I receive from the world (open centers), I knew I'd been sacrificing myself. I had also learned to listen to the energies of others, rather than my own.

For most of life, I felt disconnected from myself. I lived and operated from my head rather than feeling and honoring the emotions in my body. Trusting myself was difficult because I was conditioned to listen to others instead. I learned to follow along and fit in even if my face burned with embarrassment and my gut lurched. Those horrible feelings inside my body attempted to guide me. However, I simply ignored them, overrode them, or fought them.

These are classic examples I encounter while working with my clients and their Human Design charts. Many clients who have splits in their charts, as I do, operate from the conditioned part of the split. That usually means pushing with energies that are designed to hang back (like the mind), or repressing energies meant to come forth (like emotions or the gut).

When I received the notion my family and I were to journey to Mount Shasta, I trusted. After driving a lengthy five hours, arriving in pitch black, and being met by smoke billowing out of our trailer, I remained poised. As my husband found the smoldering source of singed blankets and pillows, caused by faulty wiring in a light, our family took care. The option to sleep in our travel trailer was out. So, we adapted. We moved a mattress into the back of the truck and gathered our sleeping bags. As it turned out, the power for the town was out due to a nearby fire. This allowed the radiance of the stars to shine against the offsetting darkness.

It was purely magical. It was divinely orchestrated.

Often, life throws curveballs. It is a choice to either feel afraid of the curveball and strike out, or to trust that all is well and smack that ball out of the park. My old untrusting self would have freaked out over the fire. However, my empowered and brave trusting self went with the flow, knowing there was something in it for me. And wow! Having the sky above me all lit with stars was an absolute, tremendous gift.

To get to this place of trust has been part of my lifelong journey. As of this writing, I've been deeply experimenting with my Design for over eight years. Feeling like I was separated within myself drove me toward *inner*standing the polarity of what I need, which is the energies of other humans to connect my chart. Specifically, this is my husband's energies whose gates bridge those apparently "separate" aspects of myself.

Here's the thing about separation. It's everywhere and nowhere all at once. Separation is in every particle of creation in our world. It's in our systems. It's in our societies. It's in our relationships. It's in our hearts. Yet, it is all an illusion.

It's not real—not physically anyway. It's something we have created to slingshot ourselves back to oneness: oneness within ourselves; oneness with each other; oneness with Mother Earth; oneness with Source/God/Creator.

Sadly, our moment of birth is exactly where that illusion begins. It is your destiny to come into form as a tiny angel and bring love and wholeness to the planet. You've chosen this destiny and you're excited. Once you come through your mother's birthing canal, the veil of separation shrouds you and you forget who you are. You struggle to remember that you *are* the light, you are connected to ALL, and are therefore, more powerful than you know.

It's ironic because *be*ing prosperous is your birth right. Yet the moment you are born, you no longer *feel* you are the essence of prosperity. Your whole life you seek prosperity because the illusion drives you to believe you are not. It's like at the start of life, you are on a boomerang trajectory of a scarce and separate path. You feel alone and without. Those feelings prove your very situation, not your destiny. Once you hit a pivotal point on your life path, the boomerang arcs its way back, propelling you towards your differing yet true reality, where you discover more of your purpose—that you are whole and prosperous.

My husband, Mike, is a single-definition three-centers Projector. Based on his unique Design, when I am with him, he energetically completes me. He is the very bridge I have sought my whole life. Through him, my mind, heart, and emotional energies unite as one.

Although I am destined to be guided by my emotions, my conditioning taught me to ignore them and listen to my mind instead. My boomerang trajectory was to be intellectual rather than feeling. I achieved many goals my mind created for me like receiving all A's in school, graduating college with a master's degree, choosing a career in the financial industry, and pushing to work harder and smarter.

It was all a path I thought I had to do alone. A path where I pushed myself like a Generator to continue achieving even when there was no invitation. Even when I lacked the energy. Even when I didn't want to. Even while stuffing down my emotions that constantly bubbled up to remind me that my true path was *not* the one I was on.

It took meeting my husband to find my way home. He has been the catalyst to me finding *me*. In Human Design, it is taught that Projectors need invitations for the big things in life: career, relationships, moving, etc. Society often says those are the biggest changes that bring considerable challenges and stresses into our lives.

Yet within two years of meeting Mike, and when my lengthy divorce was finalized, we married, he took on raising my Projector daughter, we birthed a set of Generator twins, and we purchased a home. As two Projectors, we did all the things, all at once.

We clearly embarked on an accelerated ascension journey. One where we both chose to grow from within and together. We chose family and oneness over separation, prosperity and love over scarcity.

With a split in my chart, I appreciate that Mike's Human Design naturally releases my feeling of separation. Through his energy, my two parts become fully alive and operate as one. My ability to be on purpose and trusting of myself is truly activated. I venture forward with excitement because the whole of me knows what it feels like to trust my mental *and* emotional parts.

Separation affects all of us. As a tiny human, you *feel* like you've lost your Source Love-Light connection. I am telling you that you don't really lose it. But that feeling is so strong, you believe it to be real. Remember, it is an illusion.

Part of your purpose in life is to remember—to find your way back to remembering you are one with ALL *and* to see the polarity of your path. Wherever you thought you had to go, it was the illusion keeping you from your purpose. When people proclaimed you were terrible at something, you were actually great! You learned to believe the opposite. You were then pushed into a world of situations proving that the external influences were correct, and you were wrong.

It's time to flip it all around. It's time to recognize your purpose through your hidden powers.

I feared my emotions. I heard the world tell me not to be emotional. That meant I trusted *others* more than I trusted myself. I let the external noise grow so loud that I dimmed my own light and gifts.

Through the feeling of separation within myself, it was easy to pit myself against myself. My mind would command me to turn off my emotions, so I did. My emotions would rear up during decisions, and I'd doubt my mind. I would in effect harm myself mentally with negative thoughts, and emotionally through suppression.

It's no wonder at the tender age of twelve, during my parents 'separation and divorce, I created exercise-induced asthma for myself. I didn't know how to talk about my feelings. I didn't know how to share my thoughts. What I thought and felt stayed locked inside me. That act alone took a toll on me, especially my lungs where I suddenly couldn't breathe when I played sports.

Beneath our physical, emotional, and mental ailments is Source energy. Energy is the root of all. It is the undercurrent to our very essence and being. This is why I love Human Design. At a basic level, Human Design paints the picture of how we give and receive energy in the world.

With an undefined Throat, I never felt heard and seen. I'd share insights and brilliance with others who didn't value it. I quickly learned to keep my voice silent. That meant my mind and emotions had no outlet to expel the energies within me, so they stayed stuck inside tormenting my physical body.

On an energetic level, it makes sense that our lungs tie into our emotions. When we suppress how and what we feel, we constrict our own ability to breathe in the very life force energy that sustains us. When we can't breathe, our body begins to deteriorate since it's not receiving the oxygen it needs to stay healthy. The lungs have a beautiful relationship with the heart. The heart needs the oxygen, for without it, it too will stop pumping the blood in the body. Both of these magnificent organs live in the chest.

Without blood flow and oxygen, humans cease to physically exist. On an energetic level, long before the physical body breaks down, it is the blocks in our heart chakra that result in stagnant energy. In nature, we find stagnation in pockets of dormant water. Where there's zero movement, infestations of mosquitoes and disease come in.

Energetically, if you have blocks in your chakras, your physical body creates disease. This is what I created for myself. I created the illusion where I felt alone and incapable of sharing my emotional and mental blocks. My physical body then manifested a perfect storm of symptoms proving I couldn't breathe. Because breath is life, I was no longer truly alive and on purpose.

It took me over ten years to heal my asthma and ditch the inhaler. Forgiveness was a huge piece that got me there. I had to turn inward and recognize where I was holding pain and blame in my heart. It was heaviness that shallowed my breath, so I had to release it. I chose to forgive my father and stepmother. I chose to forgive myself.

Wherever you've felt wronged in your life, there is a lesson to learn. There is a damp, dark corner in your heart or body that is infested with disease. Dis-ease is guiding you to look towards the pain, not run from it. It has a message for you. Are you willing to explore the depths of your Human Design to remember who you are? Are you willing to move towards that darkness to find your light?

The thing with polarity is that we need both aspects. We create the dance from one extreme to the other as a sense of direction to help us see where we are and don't want to be, and where we may choose to go.

Emotions absolutely work this way for me too. When I am unhappy, my emotions show me I am moving further away from what I want so it's time to stop and turn the car around. The more I have learned to listen to my emotions, the faster they give me resolve. They are my guiding light, and they are brilliant! I cry with intensity, or I simply connect and feel the emotional energy within.

The reason I have found this unity within myself is because I am surrounded by loved ones who support me being *me*. Mike unifies me so I feel that oneness of heart, body, and mind. My mind and feelings dance as one, contemplating the feelings and what they mean. They allow me to fully trust all parts of myself so my dance with polarity can be collapsed into neutrality. That's my take anyway.

I am grateful Human Design has allowed me to deeply trust myself and my inner knowing. I've become more powerful in sharing my Projector guiding abilities and innate skills so I can cross the invisible boundaries of what is possible. Through my work, I trust I am the bridge to the budding future in the financial industry, where numbers and energy dance in harmony, where humanity embraces currency rather than monetary creations through *be*ing the value the world needs, and where prosperity shows up through trusting, being, and taking aligned action using Strategy and intuition. This knowing has awakened in me because I know my Design and purpose.

We are in accelerated times of change with a mass ascension of consciousness on the planet. This means our ways of *doing* are shifting because our ways of *being* have shifted. I liken this to the transition between our focused, *doing* left brains, to the *being* ways of our right brains. It is possible to allow the right-brain, feminine aspects of creativity, receiving, flowing, waiting, and feeling, to guide us into the future rather than forcing the masculine left-brain tactics of logic, giving, structure, pushing, and thinking ways of the past.

It's a massive shift for all of us. And it's possible because *you* are the essence of prosperity.

I light up with a glowing smile of certainty when I trust I am right where I'm meant to be, *be*ing who I AM here to *be*. The glorious night sky reminds me of that. Because I AM one with the cosmos. Because I AM here on the planet living on purpose.

When each of us steps onto our own path of purpose, we light the way for others to do the same. Trust yourself. Trust your knowing. Move from I ACT to I AM through the power of trust.

You've got this! As I share with all of my clients, you are healthy, whole, perfect, prosperous, and complete. Thank you for *be*ing you. I love you.

Alana Heim

Cosmic Prosperity Activator, Certified Public
Accountant, Certified Financial Planner®,
Quantum Alignment System™ Certified

1/3 Orchestrator (Emotional Two-Motors Projector)

Alana Heim is the owner and essence of Prosperity Alignment, Inc. She serves in a unique role of being a Cosmic Prosperity Activator guiding her clients to navigate the energetic currents beneath their work, life, and money. This support allows them to naturally flow in the river of infinite prosperity. Alana is a CPA and CFP® who pairs her experience with out-of-the-box thinking, Human Design expertise, Quantum Alignment System training, neo-shamanic remote energy healing, sound channeling, and intuitive wisdom. She helps you to transform your relationships with self and money.

Alana is a four-time bestselling contributing author to *Abundance By Design: Discover Your Unique Code for Health, Wealth, and Happiness with Human Design*; *What's Money Got to Do With It?*; *Stop Overworking and Start Overflowing: 25 Ways to Transform Your Life Using Human Design;* and *The Energy Medicine Solution.*

In Human Design terms, Alana always has something to get done (undefined Root), with less time than she thinks (undefined Spleen), taking on more work than she should (undefined Sacral), with lots to say (undefined Throat), while flowing in whatever direction hits her (undefined Identity).

Alana is a 1/3 Emotional two-motors Projector. She loves honoring herself, valuing herself, trusting herself, and teaching others to do the same. She enjoys sharing her gifts in an aligned-wait-for-timing-and-recognition way. She lives in Reno, Nevada with her 4/1 Self Projector husband and their three children, a 5/1 Emotional Projector daughter, and a set of girl-boy 6/2 Emotional Generator twins.

You're invited to connect with Alana at:

ProsperityAlignment.com

Graced by Design

Elenique Marie Pizziolo

As I child of the seventies, I grew up during a time when the tension was felt between the social rules and traditions of the past and the push to create something new. In my early years, I witnessed how the old ways were still very much at the center of my family's and community's lives, and there was an incredible pressure to conform and belong.

However, every so often, we caught wind of a small rebellion. A sort of coup against the expectations and prescriptions we had been raised with. These insurgencies would be discussed at family gatherings, over hushed murmurings around the dinner table. There, all manner of imminent revolutions would be discussed, such as that of an aunt that had refused to marry and was living with her boyfriend, or the cousin who was openly gay, or that of the son who refused to take over the family business.

Although there was an element of shock and outrage in their voices, I could sense there was something more important beneath the conversation. I later recognized that what was there was fear mingled with expectancy, like watching the wave of a tsunami coming in while standing at the shore.

The tipping point of the old-world order had begun, and when I observe the world around me now, I am amazed at the fluidity of beliefs and norms of our present world. Yet I couldn't imagine that then.

Back then, I didn't know that I was a Projector being raised by not one, but two, Manifesting Generators. Unaware of Human Design or of the monumental evolutionary shift of the planet, I had no understanding of why I was so different, so out of place, and frankly, *so tired.*

Since a very early age, I always felt myself to be quite different. I had a deep sense that something very important was missing and I remember asking questions, such a wide array of questions that I would inevitably exhaust and bewilder my parents.

I was a weird little kid, fascinated and enraptured with the idea of God and wanting to understand everything about the world around me. The ultimate why of this life was foremost in my thoughts much to the confusion and frustration of those around me.

I remember being told infinitely that I needed to ask fewer questions, to just take things as they were, and not challenge everything or everyone to a duel. Being raised Catholic, the curiosity soon trickled over into the lives of saints and mystics and the powerful symbols of Jesus and Mary as models of what to aspire to.

As a voracious reader I devoured books on everything. From the Marian apparitions to the *Unbearable Lightness of Being*, I looked for answers to the why and the how. I did not know what road would get me there, but I was determined to find the source that seemed to beckon me from deep within.

What I wouldn't understand until decades later was that this drive to understand was not a punishment or a curse, but the result of an undefined Head Center whose constant pressure to figure it all out was just part of my beautiful Design.

Therefore, this was not an easy time, and growing up feeling so different from everyone else was isolating and lonely. I was simply not interested in the things that most of my friends and family were, and in response and out of necessity, I developed a persona, my own avatar, to operate in the outside world.

On the outside, I seemed to be well adjusted, a good student, a "normal" girl in the world with crushes on boys, insecurities, and a deep desire to fit in. Yet deeper within was the real me. This was a single-minded being whose only concern was to make contact with the *Why*. As the years went by without finding this, the tension between the real me and my avatar became more and more intense.

Although the people around me had their struggles, they seemed happy enough with things as they were. They expressed hopes of financial abundance, planned for their perfect home, and dreamed of the perfect relationship. Yet I had this knowing within me that even if I found all those things, the void inside of *me* would persist. I knew my longing would not be filled with the prizes of the world and a deeper sense of alienation began to grow.

Little did I know that as a 6/2 Line, I was meant to feel all these things. I didn't know I was going to have a rough first thirty years, that I would learn by making "mistakes," that I had to go through the heartache, the disappointment, the loneliness, to cultivate the learnings that would serve me later in life.

I wish I'd known that all of it would one day serve a purpose, and that, in fact, going through all these things was part of the unfolding of that purpose, because as a 6/2 Projector, I was not here to *do* but to *be*. My life was polishing me into my divine contribution, which was not an act of doing but of being. *My* purpose was to live in an aligned and authentic way and to inspire others to do the same.

Yet I was years from knowing this, and in my teens, I tried to discuss these emotions with friends and family, but over time, I soon realized that most people had no idea what I was talking about.

A heaviness began to come over me and I felt as if I was swimming in quicksand. The feeling of being so misunderstood and alone pained me deeply and I secluded into myself and accepted that I would have to carry this burden alone. This pain eventually led me into a deep depression during my teens and early adulthood.

I learned to hide it and wore a mask for the world. I perfected that art of talking about what other people wanted to talk about or hear and avoided talking about what made them uncomfortable. I pushed myself to be in the world, of the world, and set the same goals as those around me. I tried to excel, to be liked, to be helpful, and to be productive.

Yet, with every passing year, I became more and more exhausted. Keeping up the appearance of belonging was becoming an infinitely heavy task, and I often remembered the story of poor Sisyphus. Like him, I felt that every day I was rolling the world up a mountain only to find it at my feet again the next morning.

Yet despite a sense of hopelessness, something in me kept believing that an answer would come. Like a weed pushing its way through concrete, a sense of faith sustained me. When I became a mother, I knew that part of the answer had arrived. The feeling of wholeness and connection that I felt when I saw my son for the first time is indescribable.

At that moment, I knew that what I had been missing was *this* feeling, for which I didn't have a name. I now know this was the experience of unconditional love, unsullied by expectation, brilliant as the sun, peaceful as the rain. His birth was my rebirth, and I knew there was a better way to love and a freedom which he was here to teach me.

My son Noah was born with digestive problems that seemed to have no cause or diagnosis. In the beginning, we were told he would grow out of them, yet as the years went by, and we cycled in and out of hospitals as if through a revolving door, the answers failed to come.

We were told that there was a possibility that he might have a rare genetic disorder, but we wouldn't be able to test for it until he was older and could have the biopsy needed to confirm it.

In my desperation to help him, I began to deepen my knowledge of healing. I studied faith healing, energy healing, crystal healing, Reiki, Pranic Healing, and many more to help him.

As I studied these, I began to understand the importance of vibration and mindset. I began to see the critically important link between our thoughts, beliefs, emotions, and the world outside of us. I knew that to help Noah, I would have to rewire myself. I threw myself diligently into the task and created all kinds of practices and protocols so I could facilitate a healing space for him. I understood that I could only channel energy equal to my vibration, so I worked on myself and waited for a miracle.

When he turned nine years old, we flew to Ohio to a world-renowned children's hospital where the best specialists in pediatric digestive diseases practiced. After performing extensive biopsies and after enduring what seemed an endless two-week wait, we received the results. He didn't have it! A miracle had been granted.

While they determined that the cause of his constipation was idiopathic, meaning it had no visible cause, they said he did not have the genetic disorder they had feared. He was "normal" and for the first time in his life he was told he could eat whatever he wanted as long as he followed a pretty simple protocol to make sure he went to the bathroom regularly and kept the gut bacteria in check.

The diagnosis was the fulfillment of a prayer that had formed on my lips since the time he was days old and which I had whispered every day of his life. As we returned home triumphantly, we all settled into our new life and our new future with unparalleled joy. And it was joy that overflowed as we watched him play soccer, eat his favorite meals, and hang out with his friends knowing that for the first time in his life, we didn't need to fear losing him.

We drank life in, cautiously optimistic that his illness was behind us. Then, one afternoon in December 2018, I picked him up from school and together with my youngest son, we headed to McDonald's. This was a rare treat since we tried to keep his diet as clean as possible. Yet when we arrived at the drive thru, he didn't want anything. I was shocked because it was one of his favorite treats. I knew something was wrong and left the drive thru line and headed home.

Just a few hours later I found myself on the balcony of the Saint Elisabeth Hospital in Curaçao, in the early morning hours of December 13, 2018, watching six doctors with heads downcast coming towards me from the operating room.

"We're so sorry. He didn't make it."

The words were spoken out loud, but they felt more like they had crystallized into a knife that pierced my heart into a kaleidoscope of pieces. As the world of color and sound drifted further and further away from me, I realized I, too, was dying. As sick as he had been for the first seven years of his life, the last two years had lulled me into a sense of safety. I had slowly opened the drawers of my life and put away my fear, replaced my armor with a cape of hope, unlocked my heart to hear it sing in praise, and left myself wide open for the unthinkable. And now it was here with no warning and no mercy.

As I walked backwards towards the railing, I heard a scream escape from my lips, but it seemed as if I wasn't the one uttering it. I held the railing in my hands and looked over at the street below. It was only four stories up, but it was high enough. I heard myself think, *I need to go with him* and felt my grip around the rail tighten. I felt myself pull back as if to have momentum with which to cast myself over the rail when a voice broke through my thoughts. The voice was in my head and yet it wasn't mine and it simply said, "Okay, if you want to jump, then jump. But realize that if you do, you take all of them with you."

As I looked to my right, I could suddenly see an image of my whole family. In front was my youngest son Nicolas and then my husband, my parents, and many more people whose faces I couldn't see. It was like a carnival mirror that went on forever.

Something in me knew right then and there that a greater force than me was asking me to make a choice. I knew whatever I chose would be hard. If I left, it would be hard on them; if I stayed, it would be hard on me. I also knew that if I stayed, it could not be as a shadow of myself for this would just be greater torture for all of us.

I knew the decision to live in a world without my boy was unthinkable and yet it was being presented to me. I don't know why, but I could feel it was some sort of invitation. I now know this to be the beginning of my greatest lesson, the sorrow that would transform my life, the loss that would give it meaning, the teacher that would lead the way. It is what calls me to write these words today. For I now realize that the transformation of this sorrow into service is the purpose of my journey, and I hope that it is helpful in some way.

The next few days and weeks were—and still are—a complete blur. I would wake up every morning believing that I had awoken from a nightmare only to discover that the nightmare was real. I was numb and it seemed to me that I was watching myself from some very far away place. My mind had gone somewhere deep into hiding and what remained was a combination of conditioned automatic responses and something new.

At the time I wasn't certain what it was. It was a kind of calm—a presence that was with me as soon as I opened my eyes. Yet it was also there when I closed them. This knowing was next to me and within me and outside of me, even in the wind. I slowly began to understand that I wasn't alone. My son was not physically with me any longer, but something had come to take his place. Something had come to hold my hand. It was as if my soul, every cell of my being, was being carried on the energy of something larger than myself. From the moment of his passing, I began to hear my son's voice in my mind. He would tell me what I needed to do to make it through the minutes, then the hours, and then the days.

Yet, while surrendering to the guidance had offered me a way to survive, it wasn't without its challenges. We don't just stop being who we've been—overnight. My pre-existing pattern of needing to be in control coupled with my grief, took on a dimension of its own. It was as if I was two people, the one who I had been and the one I was becoming.

Despite "surrendering," I still found myself on an emotional rollercoaster and the range of feelings I experienced in those first twelve months were like meeting every permutation of myself that had ever existed or would ever exist. It was as if I was phasing in and out of reality, never sure which version of me would show up. The shock of losing Noah had pried open all the locks on the doors of my defenses and an avalanche of buried emotions burst up from deep within me. I was holding court with the best and the worst of myself and I wasn't sure who would win in the end.

All the shadows that we hide from are suddenly set free in the vacuum that grief provides. The trickiest part of grief is that you spend most of your time at war with yourself. An exhausting tug-of-war ensues where a part of you wants to feel better and happy again while simultaneously, another part of you believes nothing will ever be okay again. In fact, you believe nothing *should* be okay again because if it is, it means you have forgotten the one that you've lost.

I once read that guilt is the most damaging emotion. Yet the grief and guilt of outliving your child is the worst kind of torture.

The inner voice kept saying I needed to surrender but I had little idea of what that truly meant. I could feel that something needed to change but I didn't know what. My mind scrambled back and forth, like a trapped animal, looking for a plan. But a plan for what? When you don't know what you want it's hard to make a plan. What *can* you want after you lose your child? What new dream can you come up with that makes any sense?

Deep inside, you sense there shouldn't even be a world anymore. This world and all its goals, pleasures, sorrows, challenges, opportunities, tragedies, seems—at its core— meaningless. If the world can go on without Noah, what's the point of the world?

I realized then I needed to let the world die if I was going to go on living. The whole structure of reality needed a serious reboot. The reality that made up the world I had inhabited until then needed to be undone. Without knowing it, my sorrow was calling forth a brave new world.

Like Neo from *The Matrix*, I was sitting in front of a choice. If I chose the blue pill, I could go on "living" the life I'd known, I could occupy some broken version of myself, held together by the cast of sorrow. I didn't know how long I could make it like that, but it required that I stop thinking and feeling and just go on "living."

If I took the red pill, I would wake up in Wonderland, in an unknown territory, limited only by my resolve and my imagination. *What would that look like? Would it be any better?* Something in me knew that once the question entered my mind, so did the answer. I had no intention of staying in a world without Noah, so I would make a new one where he and everything eternal was the new normal. Feeling hopeful for the first time in months, my experiment with building a new world began.

What does it take to make a new world? First, let the old one die. This involves abandoning the old ways of thinking, being, and believing. I knew I needed to tap into something greater than myself and I decided I wouldn't give up until I found it. This is the most monumental decision I have ever made because it completely altered the course and nature of my life.

Step one was to seriously commit to meditation and surrender. I knew my own energy wouldn't get me there. I needed to allow for something greater to carry me. Since he passed away, I could hear Noah speaking to me and his messages always seemed to point me in the same direction. "Go sit for meditation Mama" or "Come in the garden and feel the wind move." I could sense that he was asking me to go outside my normal routines and limits. It was a call to be present, to be in the moment, and to allow that moment to offer me something.

I would sometimes be drawn to a book on the shelf, or a video would show up on YouTube which would offer some unexpected guidance or answer a question. This is precisely how I found Human Design. I followed the breadcrumbs and the more I listened and followed the instructions, the more the guidance came.

I started to realize that following guidance was a matter not only of trust but also of habit. Just as I had learned to perceive the world around me in a certain way and to believe that this was "reality," I began to see that my perception of the world was also a consequence of habit.

I wanted to see the world with fresh eyes and this desire called forth the guidance that led me to Human Design. I remember having my first reading listening to the words whose meaning I'd been waiting to hear my whole life:

"You are a Projector Type. You are here to guide others and to hold the blueprint for the world. You might have felt that growing up you didn't fit in and didn't think like other people. That's because you've come to anchor change. You are a change agent. You are here to anchor the light. That means that you do not have your own sustainable energy force. You are not meant to work as others do because you cannot sustain your energy the way they can."

Tears filled my eyes as I heard her words. It was if I was being seen for the very first time in my life. For the first time, there was someone who could understand and express my differentness, my loneliness, my exhaustion, and my calling.

As I explored my chart, I began to understand myself in ways I never knew possible. Human Design offered me the grace to accept myself as I am and to step into my power. It provided me with the framework with which to understand not only myself but also my family and my friends.

This understanding has brought so much healing and forgiveness to my relationship with myself and with others.

Human Design has given me an empowering paradigm with which to understand my humanity, the world, and everyone it. It has also been instrumental in helping me navigate my grief by helping me understand my unique needs and challenges during the grieving process.

I realized that while other people might need and want the company of others while grieving, as a Projector and 6/2 Profile, I needed solace and silence to process my pain.

With an open Emotional Solar Plexus, I noticed that when I was around others, I would pick up and magnify their sadness within me. This left me more depressed and burned out, yet I felt guilty to admit this or express this to anyone. I felt I had a responsibility to be there for the people who needed me even when it was wearing me out.

Yet once Human Design helped me understand who I was and what I needed to operate in an optimal way, I was able to release the guilt and set healthy boundaries for myself.

Instead of hurting those around me, the result of this act of self-love and self-understanding was that I began to heal and recover more and more each day. Therefore, I was able to be there for my friends and loved ones in a much deeper way because I was finally in alignment with myself.

The most difficult moments of our lives are inviting us to recognize the powerful and unique beings that we truly are. Human Design is a bridge that helps us to uncover the unique strengths and gifts that we bring into this world. When we remember who we really are, we activate the highest expression of our Design. It is this expression that allows us to feel pain yet not remain in suffering, to experience challenge but to learn to rise above it.

If you're struggling with grief or loss, I want to encourage you to keep going. If you're reading this book, then an answer to your prayers and questions has found you. By utilizing Human Design to understand and honor yourself and your process, you cease to be a victim to the world and become the architect of your own life.

I am forever transformed by the healing this journey—and Human Design—has offered me and am eternally grateful to my Noah for guiding me to the answers I was always seeking.

I now realize that becoming myself *is* my purpose. I am my own work of art; I am the path I was seeking and the destination; I am the answer and the question. Human Design taught me that I am here to serve by owning my experiences, transforming my pain and challenges, stepping into my light, and shining it as a beacon that reminds others that what is within me is also in them.

They too are miraculous creations and have the power to endure, to transform, to overcome, and to step into their wildly beautiful purpose with confidence and trust.

We are all expressions of the one Source; we are all the light expressing. We are all that love and as Noah whispered to me once in a dream, "Everything is love Mom. *Everything is love.*"

Elenique Marie Pizziolo

Clinical Hypnotherapist, Author, Human Design
Specialist, and Spiritual Mentor

6/2 Orchestrator (Projector)

Elenique Marie is a clinical hypnotherapist, energy therapist, and spiritual mentor who utilizes Human Design, energy psychology, and hypnotherapy to help her clients remember and awaken to the power of who they truly are and what they're here to do. For over fifteen years, she has been teaching, speaking, and coaching clients to achieve transformational change.

She also co-hosts the *Miraculous Thinking* podcast where she breaks down well-known spiritual texts and esoteric wisdom into easy to understand and implementable strategies.

Elenique Marie is devoted to helping people remember the power of their authentic self by helping them undo the conditioning and limiting beliefs that are keeping them from experiencing the true greatness and power of their unique Design. Her passion is to guide people in their reawakening so they can create the life they've always wanted with ease, authenticity, and joy.

Elenique is the mother of two incredible boys who have taught her everything she knows about love. She is a wife to her best friend, and when she's not working, you can find her cooking passionately or reading quietly. She has a BA in theology and economics from Wellesley College in Massachusetts and is a lifelong learner. She is an ordained minister and some of her other certifications include clinical hypnotherapist, Quantum Human Design Specialist, and EFT and Master NLP Practitioner. She knows that part of her life's purpose is to help people remember, reclaim, and experience the power, beauty, and uniqueness of who they truly are.

Elenique believes that as human beings on the planet right now, we are being invited to heal ourselves and to constantly evolve our understanding. Human Design and hypnosis are powerful keys that open the doors to self-knowledge, which allow us to awaken and thrive. If you'd like to explore ways that you can step into and live your purpose by design, you can connect with her on her website.

Eleniquemarie.com

Follow Elenique Marie on Instagram @eleniquemariecoaching

and on YouTube at

Youtube.com/c/EleniqueMarie

Not Broken, Perfect; And So Are You

By Grace Gravestock

How Human Design Found Me

About a month after having been laid off, which was just two months after my divorce was final, I started the day in the worst possible way. I looked in the mirror and saw a squishy-looking body much larger than I remembered ever being. My head was pounding, and the migraine felt so miserable that I just wanted to die. *I'm ready to check out*, I thought, as my new housemate's incessantly cheerful smile greeted me in the kitchen. He asked me how I slept, and I began to sob quietly.

It felt like just too much pain. Losing my marriage after fifteen years, getting laid off right after the divorce was final, and now facing debilitating headaches that had wracked my body for eighteen years felt like too much, and my body was exhausted.

"You're going to get through this," he said. "I promise you; life will get way better."

The tone of his words somehow gave me confidence that my feelings were temporary and as we talked, I realized my intention would determine whether this was the best or worst thing that ever happened to me.

Sick and tired of being the victim, I made a conscious decision: "I will survive, and I will thrive." Shortly after this conversation, I finally gave in to my friend's insistence that I get a Human Design reading.

The reading was several hundred dollars, and I was not used to spending that kind of money on myself. Because I had paid so much, I took it very seriously. On the third time I listened to the recording, while transcribing, suddenly, the light bulb in my head went off: *blink, blink, blink.* I heard in my head *You are not broken. You don't need to be fixed, and you are perfectly designed to be and do exactly what you're here to be and do.* That revelation changed my life forever.

The Missing Component in Personal Change Management

As a professional change manager for more than fifteen years, I was proud of the career I'd worked hard to build. Large-scale technology implementations for blue-chip companies and governments had become familiar as I moved from project to project, helping leaders make big changes more palatable to their teams through engagement, communications, and training. Sometimes this meant laying people off, since as technology improved, fewer and fewer people were needed to get things done.

I decided to apply the change management tools, techniques, and processes to my own personal life changes. What I realized in frustration, was that the missing component was *energy.* Even while working with some of the smartest people in the world, no one had ever spoken about frequency or energy as a component of change management.

Learning about Human Design piqued my interest in energy and frequency. I realized that everything has an energetic frequency, much like a radio station. Though I've always been a positive person, I realized that because I had been living from obligation rather than desire, my life could be measured on the same plane as a low frequency of fear. I recognized that I needed to raise my vibration to make change easier to adopt.

As my frequency shifted, the changes in my personal life were much easier to adopt and my relationships began to shift in a favorable way too. One of the key inputs to my understanding of frequency and its impact was through the book *Power vs. Force* (Hay House Inc., 2014) and The Hawkins Scale, which illustrates the relative frequency scale of emotional states, as described by David R. Hawkins, MD, PhD, a widely known authority within the fields of consciousness research and spirituality. This scale, ranging from one to seven hundred, designates numbers for emotions. Hawkins puts fear at one hundred and love at five hundred and illustrates that when you are in fear you are in a state of contraction and just getting by, but when you are in a state of love, you are expanded and approaching ultimate consciousness and enlightenment.

For a while, I became an energy healer to learn about the subtle body energy field and then I shifted my energy by changing my beliefs and letting go of what no longer served:

- I replaced fear with love.
- I replaced obligation with desire.
- I replaced security based in external factors with security based on trusting myself.
- I replaced emotional attachments to people, places, things, or ideas with real-time loving connections in the moment.
- Because expectation creates attachments, which can lead to disappointment and pain, I replaced that with anticipation derived from love and trust and preceding from openness.
- I replaced emotional attachments, which come from fear, with discernment, focused on the facts.
- I replaced commitments based in obligation (e.g., no escape clause) with commitments based in desire (e.g., an agreement or understanding).
- I realized that fixing or changing the other is unsustainable and always ends in failure, so I replaced it with accepting the other as they are and loving them unconditionally.
- I stopped taking responsibility for others and putting others before my own well-being. I started taking personal responsibility and sole ownership of my life and stopped blaming others.

These energetic shifts took time to understand, accept, and embody but the more I learned about my true nature through Human Design, the easier it became to let go of conditioning and programming and choose more empowering beliefs and practices. As I practiced Human Design to learn to love myself and implemented self-care, I also rebuilt my belief system. I explored many practical ways to support my new life and higher frequency including essential oils, live and enzyme-rich raw foods, energy medicine, and a variety of practices including meditation.

Raising Frequency with a Gratitude Journal

As I experimented with practical ways to raise my frequency, what resonated most was the power of gratitude. I learned firsthand that it could quickly help me shift my attitude and mindset and even create intentionally by becoming a frequency match to that which I wanted to create. Before I returned to professional change management and executive coaching, I read more than two thousand charts and helped many women in transition create a life they wanted to live by learning about their own value through their unique Human Design energy blueprint. One of the first and most powerful assignments I still give my coaching clients is to begin a gratitude journal practice.

To start, you need just five minutes per day plus a pen and paper. It helps to do this morning and evening, but the most important thing is to get started and do it regularly because the process conditions your energy field and helps you to attract what you want into your life through repetition. Once you have become an energetic match, you will attract those things.

It's a two-step process that starts with writing this: "I am so happy and grateful that …" and then complete the sentence with at least three things you're genuinely grateful for in the moment and why. This helps you determine what you want to increase in your life. By doing this, you're acknowledging that you're already in abundance (which is a frequency), and you're gaining clarity on what you want to create more of. Just by focusing on it and committing to writing each day, you'll start to see patterns.

Like most of my clients, I have struggled with knowing what I want to create in my life but committing to this daily gratitude practice helps me to see what is working, what makes me feel good, and, therefore, what I want to see increase. Also important is raising frequency with gratitude so that you can begin to create consciously and intentionally in the next step.

The second part sounds the same but is different. Again, you write "I'm so happy and grateful that …" but this time you fill in the blanks with what you don't yet have but want to have (this is to help you determine *what* to create—it's important that you're not coming from a "lack" frequency), and what you can genuinely feel grateful for *now*, as if it's already yours.

Each of these elements helps you tap into the quantum field of infinite possibilities to claim something specific that you are choosing to bring into your own 3D field with intention.

It's very important to feel the emotion that is a frequency match to what you're wanting to create because like attracts like and that brings more of it into your field. For most people, it comes in the form of something to respond to (an invitation, or an energy rush), depending on their energetic configuration. It's important to maintain the higher frequency of gratitude to create; therefore, feeling grateful *now* is key. When you feel grateful AS IF it's already yours, you are claiming it and becoming an energetic match. There's an older "name it to claim it" technique that's associated with manifesting and it's popular because the more specific you can be, the more likely it is that you'll become an energetic match and therefore manifest what you want to create.

Living in Alignment Helped Me Create the Life I Wanted

I am here to lead by example and because I've been able to successfully create a whole new life since my own midlife transition, I know it's possible for my clients.

When you start to see that you've created what's showing up in your life and that you've created it *because* you are a powerful being, you begin to understand how limitless you really are! My intention for all my clients is freedom: Stop giving your power away, and instead stand in your full power to intentionally create a life consciously and that you WANT to live!

When you begin to truly live in alignment with your Design—what you are literally configured to be and do—you are BEing yourself, and you can also then choose what affects you. Once you can choose what affects you, you're no longer subject to being controlled or manipulated by anyone's behavior or circumstances that used to determine your mood or experiences. You become so strong and in control of your own power that others can no longer siphon it off.

Taking Back My Power and Ending Headaches Through Self-Care

As I learned about my own Human Design, I realized that it was helping me to know and love myself, and because I loved myself—finally, for the first time in my life—I learned to practice self-care.

The debilitating migraine headaches finally went away when I put a self-care practice in place. After months without a headache, I realized that for more than eighteen years, my body had been trying to give me a message through the pain: I was living someone else's life, and I was out of alignment with my Design. I had spent decades and tens of thousands of dollars trying to change myself, believing that there was something wrong with me. For most of our fifteen-year marriage, my ex had reinforced the message that I was broken, and that is why we had no sex. As it turned out, he was living in fear of accepting his own true nature and projected on me to keep his secret life quiet. Full of conditioning and programming about "'til death do us part," we stayed in an unhealthy and very unsatisfying marriage out of obligation, not desire.

Finally learning about and practicing self-care and how my chronic headaches were a message to wake up, was a valuable lesson that I learned after *many* years of trying "everything" to "cure" them. Please consider this possibility for you or someone you know who also suffers from chronic pain.

What had worked when drugs, supplements, and so many other things didn't work to get rid of my headaches? It was a self-care routine of consistent yoga, meditation, and strength training that took time and effort but made me feel good in my body. This self-care routine helped me finally achieve the muscular and fit body I had always dreamed of having. And in the process, I noticed that my headaches disappeared.

Human Design helped me to stop giving away my power and, in fact, it helped me take back my power by living in alignment with my Design. Our Design gives us a roadmap for why we're here. Defined (or colored in) centers show us what we're here to master in this life because the energy is consistent, and we have ample opportunity to use it always. Open (or white) centers show us the lessons we are here to learn, or what we are here to become wise about.

With an open Will Center, valuing myself enough to make time for regular self-care was one of the key life lessons my Human Design chart indicated. The Human Design chart represents the energetic blueprint. The open Will configuration also indicates a need to prove oneself and that explained why I felt compelled to have three jobs since I was fifteen years old (to prove that I was worthy of abundance).

Learning to put myself first is a key life lesson shown by an open Solar Plexus, and the fact that it was so challenging to make time for self-care for most of my life before Human Design, it is an indication that I was still becoming wise about that. The open Solar Plexus configuration also provides opportunities to overcome codependency, which is the lesson I had to learn by leaving my toxic marriage.

My other open center is my G Center. The life lesson of this configuration is to become wise about who to allow into my inner circle, since this center can easily absorb aspects of the other's identity. Leaving the unhealthy marriage and choosing instead to live with people who were supportive of me and living authentically, were signs that I had finally become wise about my identity. These aspects alone were enough for me to realize that Human Design could help me make sense of my life's struggles and patterns.

As I learned about my own Human Design and began doing free readings for anyone who would listen, I realized the significance and importance of following my Strategy and listening to my Inner Authority. In Human Design, *Inner Authority* is the way that you know what is correct for you. Most people have an Inner Authority based in their gut, Emotional Solar Plexus, or Spleen.

Over time, I developed an amazingly simple four-step manifestation process that has since helped me to create consciously and intentionally whatever I want in my life, usually fast.

My Four-Step Manifestation Process

1. Set a clear intention.

The first step is to set a clear intention. The main goal of this step is to have as much clarity as is needed so that when that thing or person or event comes into your life, you can recognize that you created it. When you do this, you begin to stand in your power as a creator. It helps to set an intention with a 360-degree view of what you want to create. Imagine what it looks, feels, tastes, and sounds like. It helps to imagine how you will *feel* when you have it.

The simple truth is that we are all designed to manifest, and the way to do it is just to BE a frequency match to that which we want to create. Most of us have been conditioned and programmed in ways that distort and unnecessarily hijack what in other realms is an instant process. Becoming more conscious and aware of how our thoughts, words, and intentions influence the life we're always creating can help us manifest faster and easier because then we can see when everything is in alignment (or not). Resistance in the form of incongruence is the most common roadblock to manifestation.

2. Follow your Human Design Strategy.

In Human Design, everyone has a Strategy depending on their Energy Type. There are four Energy Types for the purpose of Strategy and each one is a little bit different. Manifestors make up about 9 percent and their Strategy is to inform so they just must speak it! Generator Types make up about 70 percent of the population and their Strategy is to wait for something to respond to. That means it will be something that shows up in their physical field, something they can see, smell, taste, touch, or hear and that gives a trigger to respond to. Because Manifesting Generators are hybrids of Manifestors and Generators, they have the added step—like Manifestors (Initiators) of "seeing" and then "speaking" (or writing) what they want. This step engages the motorized Throat, which can increase the speed of the manifestation.

Projectors make up about 21 percent and they need to wait to be recognized and then invited. This ensures that they give their precious energy only to those who deserve it and for whom the exchange is a win-win. They can speed up the process by ensuring that they've prepared themselves fully for the next invitation by focusing on their self-care. Reflectors are in the minority at just 1 percent. They must wait an entire moon cycle, usually a month, before they have clarity on the direction that is correct. They are uniquely "open" and receptive to all the energies, which helps them experience the full range and perform their role of calibrating for the group.

Manifestors will follow their own internal creative flow and are meant "to inform" so they can speak what they want, informing those who will be affected by their actions. For Reflectors, the Strategy is to wait a full moon cycle. This is because they experience all the potential energy patterns in this period, and get clarity about what they want to create, over time. Spending time in nature can help any Type immensely in gaining clarity and insight when setting an aligned intention.

3. Follow your inner guidance system.

The third step is to listen to your inner GPS because it tells you what's correct *for* you and is specific *to* you.

Most people will either listen to their gut (Sacral) or wait for clarity over time (Emotional Solar Plexus) to get a yes or no about someone or something. Most others have a "knowing" that's virtually instant (Splenic). The Spleen speaks in a still small voice that, if you're not paying attention to it, you can miss. It only speaks in real-time, and it only tells you once. If your Inner Authority is Splenic, make sure that you spend time alone in quiet solitude, so you can hear your inner guidance voice. There are a couple other types of Authority that are rare (Ego Authority, No Authority, etc.) and they benefit most from listening to themselves talk about the decision they are considering, which is called the sounding board technique. It's worth knowing that they do NOT need advice when they are talking about their pending decision, but they benefit from hearing the frequency of their own voice to know what is correct.

Many people don't yet trust their inner knowing and are conditioned and programmed to make decisions from their rational minds. Human Design teaches us to listen to our bodies, and the energy centers that we call "motors" to make correct decisions rather than follow logic or reason, which are gifts made for other purposes besides personal decisions.

4. Validate your decision by checking signature.

Each Energy Type has a particular "signature" or sign that helps them know whether they're in alignment in a given moment. For Generator Types, this will feel like satisfaction, which may be experienced as having unlimited energy for a certain thing or simply feeling good. Alternatively, Generator Types will experience frustration if they are not in alignment.

Projector Types will experience either success or bitterness. Projector success is about being recognized and appreciated while bitterness can come from sharing with others who are not ready to "hear" the wisdom being offered.

Manifestor Types will experience either peace or anger. Manifestors want to be left alone in peace to create according to their own internal flow and when that flow is interrupted, they can feel what may appear to others as anger.

Reflector Types will experience either surprise or disappointment. Reflectors have a superpower of being able to see the highest potential in people or circumstances and when they see this potential actualized, they experience surprise. Also, because they so keenly see the potential, they can experience disappointment when that potential is NOT realized.

Discover Your Manifesting Strategy

There are two distinct types of manifesting strategies: either specific or nonspecific.

Specific Manifesting Strategy Example

My partner has *specific* manifesting strategy for example, and he decided he wanted a specific apartment overlooking a particular wooded area. He wanted a second-floor unit in a specific building. Against all odds, he got the apartment that he wanted, and we knew at that moment it was because he created that reality. People with a specific manifesting strategy do best to pay attention to the specific details that occur to them as they consider what to intentionally create.

Nonspecific Manifesting Strategy Example

I have *nonspecific* manifesting strategy which means that I just focus on the feeling of what I want and let the Universe surprise me with the details that are likely better than what I could have determined alone. When I manifested my partner, it was through a verbal version of the gratitude journal process. I agreed with a friend to do a ten-minute manifestation call where she had five minutes and I had five minutes to speak. When it was my turn, I said with enthusiasm and realistic energy (as if it had already happened) "I'm so happy and grateful that attractive, conscious men are lining up outside my front door to take me on fun dates." I said this because I didn't have much experience dating and I thought it'd be fun to have some fun dates! Why not? And then I said, "I also have these large chunks of money just coming in without me having to do anything!"

The very next day, not one but TWO guys asked me out and $1000 came in unexpectedly when I wasn't even working. During one of our early dates, my partner said, "I have a specific intention for our time together: I want to take you on fun dates!" No one has before or since said that, and I knew in that moment that I had manifested this relationship.

Grace Gravestock

Change Management and Frequency Mentor,
Speaker, and Podcast Host

2/5 Time Bender (Manifesting Generator)

Grace is a professional change manager turned personal transformation coach who helps women attract satisfaction and success through alignment with their purpose and highest frequency.

After years as an international change expert, consulting governments and global organizations, her "perfect" life was shattered by a divorce, layoff, downsizing, and health crisis all within a short time. Human Design helped her realize she was not broken, but perfectly designed to be and do what she is here to do. Then, while applying professional transformation tools to her own change crisis, she realized the missing component was energy. Raising her frequency was key to her and her clients' personal transformations. She achieved this by becoming a Human Design coach, dynamic speaker and trainer, change catalyst, and podcast host. Grace is here to connect, motivate, and inspire.

A recovering workaholic and parental guide to a young New Paradigm Leader, her focus is managing her vibration, traveling often, and enjoying life in Austin with her family-by-choice. She has her M.A. in transnational communication and global media and B.S. in public relations.

Grace teaches change resiliency, living in alignment with purpose, and how to maximize impact through higher frequency for better health, wealth, and purpose. Find out more at:

ActivateYourLifePurpose.com

Connect with Grace:

Linkedin.com/in/ggravestock/

and YouTube @gracegravestock

The True Awakening

By Michelle Williams

I spent my life being polite, saying yes, and conforming to others even when it didn't feel right for me. Like many, I was taught a lot of things growing up: to not rock the boat because it's not worth it; if you asked a question, you were dumb; if you pushed back, you were hard to deal with. These teachings came from many areas of my life—family, friends, schooling, religion—and as I grew older, they consumed me in unimaginable ways.

As a child, I also had an extreme fear of death. I would lie awake at night wondering why we were here, and what the point of life was. When asking about this, I was told I didn't need to worry about it right now and to just continue being a kid. This taught me that we had no reason for being here, no purpose, and that when we died, nothing happened. I felt like we were just here to have challenges and struggle in life, which made me extremely sad and caused me to feel like I didn't have value in the world. I felt disconnected from everyone and everything around me and an emptiness stayed within me most of my life.

As a result of these experiences, I lost my identity. I began to go with the flow of everyone else. As an adult, I completely changed my personality based on the person I was with. If I was dating someone, I'd act like what I thought he wanted. If I was out with a friend, I went where they wanted and had conversations that interested them but not me. Even though most of these relationships didn't last, it worked for most of my life, but as it continued, resentment and fear built up inside of me. I became resentful of myself for not standing in my power to do what made *me* happy which caused a fear that I would never be my authentic self—I didn't even know who she was.

I continued to go through life with this deep hate of self and doing what everyone else wanted. I went to college and got as much education as possible (two master's degrees) because that's what my parents and my boss wanted. I hated school with a passion and did the minimal amount possible in my classes. I searched and searched for the right guy that could fill the loneliness within me and "fix" my life. That search only caused extreme heartache and the feeling that something was wrong with me because relationships never worked out. I thought what was happening in my life just was, that it couldn't be changed and that complaining about life was *normal*.

On the exterior, I appeared happy most of the time and had all the basic material things in life that most people wanted. I had the house with a pool, nice cars, good friends, good-paying job, and freedom to do whatever I wanted, when I wanted. Friends and acquaintances told me they were jealous of the freedom I had. I never understood why because deep down I felt like I was in a prison which was preventing me from being who I really was and doing what I am in this world to do. Even though I had no idea what that purpose was, I knew it was something special; still, I had no idea how to get there.

I had a deep yearning to feel valued and purposeful in life. I wanted to feel a sense of freedom from my past and from the burdens that others put on me throughout my entire life. But the teachings from childhood were ingrained in me, and I had the belief that it wasn't possible. I thought we weren't in life to *feel*, we were in life to *do* and *be* what everyone else wanted.

The frustration of being the person everyone else wanted, built up inside of me and eventually boiled over causing a downward spiral in my life. I had health, financial, and relationship issues. I was depressed and drank each day to cover the pain and disappointment that was within me. I hid the agony from everyone else because if they knew I wasn't the "put together person" that I portrayed, I would disappoint and lose them. I was afraid if I changed who I was *acting* like, I would hurt the people around me and rock the boat, which would push everyone in my life away, leaving me alone and miserable.

More importantly, I lost trust, respect, and love for myself. Worse, I had no idea how to get it back or that I even could. I was lost. I had no purpose, courage, or direction, and I was letting fear run my life.

When I was in my early thirties, the same thoughts from when I was a child started to resurface. *Why am I here? What is my purpose?* This time, I wasn't taking someone else's word for it! I needed to understand who I was. At that time in my life, I just finished college and my job had slowed down to a normal forty-hour work week. I actually had the *time* to take the inward journey to answer these questions.

I began journaling, meditating, and studying metaphysics. During this search, I realized that I was living life all wrong. I was letting life happen *to* me and letting others control me. Just by realizing I needed to make a change, life started to shift in a positive way—literally out of nowhere. I began to change, almost forcefully, into a different person, which was terrifying yet strangely comforting. I felt like my eyes opened to the people around me and I realized some weren't true friends. I realized that I was giving so much of myself without *allowing* myself to receive anything in return. I significantly reduced drinking. Instead, I read self-help books and journaled about what I was feeling and experiencing in life.

While this seems normal to most, to me it was the complete opposite of what I used to be and because of that, I was fearful of losing the people in my life and becoming someone they didn't know. I was afraid of their judgment. I was afraid of what the future would bring if I made the changes in my life that felt right to me.

Little did I know, these changes were occurring during the time of my Saturn return—the time in life where Saturn returns to the position of our birth which can be a pretty hard nudge to help us find our true selves and our soul's purpose. The problem was, I had lived for thirty years doing what everyone else wanted and didn't know how to live any differently. I was at a crossroads.

Many people experience these feelings and have no idea what they are or how to handle them. We pretty much have two choices: go inward and find the parts of our life where we need to make changes to become more in alignment with our soul's purpose or resist, which makes life extremely difficult. Without the courage to make real changes in our life, we often let fear consume us, which keeps us in old patterns. Our life then adapts to these patterns again and we continue down the resistance path for another thirty years until we get the *get back on track!* nudge from wonderful Saturn again.

The sudden shift in my life opened something beautiful within me. I realized that I absolutely hated feeling frustrated, depressed, and not like "myself" (whoever that was). In an attempt to answer the *who are you?* question that several people had asked me, I spent several years on my journey of self-discovery, which brought me to Human Design.

I had seen Human Design in my social media feed for a while but didn't investigate what it was. It looked too complicated, and I had so many tools that were already helping me on my healing journey. I continued shifting my beliefs and deconditioning my programming which caused drastic changes in my life very quickly. When I was ready for it, I found a course on how to work with my Human Design to help my business, and I thought I'd try it out. It felt right and I instantly fell in love.

For the first time in my life, I felt understood! What I had been feeling throughout my life started to make sense. I was able to accept who I am, why I am here, and the lessons I am learning in this lifetime. I had an incredible focus point to make lasting changes in my life, and to help others do the same! I immediately absorbed as much Human Design knowledge as I could!

> *The two most important days of your life are the day you were born*
> *and the day you find out why. —Mark Twain.*

Understanding the intricate details of my Design was absolutely fascinating. It helped give me the drive and determination to bring my purpose forward. It brought back self-worth, value, and my identity.

I believe that our personalities and the lives we are creating are made of conditioning or programming that comes from multiple sources. The lessons we are to learn in this life can be influenced in many different ways, including through the people in our lives and our astrological patterns.

The Human Design chart, along with other healing modalities, and my intuitive insights have given—and continue to give—me a great understanding of where this conditioning comes from based on the definition and openness in my chart.

- Our definition (the defined, colored-in areas of the chart) is our soul contract, which is influenced by agreements we made prior to incarnation, in past lives, deep ancestral beliefs/programming, and soul level programming. These patterns are typically consistent and will repeat themselves until they are learned.
- Our openness (the undefined, non-colored or white areas of the chart) is heavily influenced by the energies around us; teachings (school, religion, etc.), group consciousness (collective, world, etc.), absorbed energies from others, genetics, environment, nature, planets, and learned behaviors and patterns throughout life. These energies and feelings typically change based on the energies in the field at

the time (people, places, media, etc.) but they create deep conditioning and belief patterns.

We unknowingly live our lives based on conditioning, and we receive more conditioning every single day. Conditioning allows us to bring patterns into our lives that challenge us and help us learn in order to grow. Many of us see these challenges as "just the way life is," which is what we are programmed to believe.

The conditioning and programming that we have within can be shifted and changed with the right techniques. It is a fun and easy process that can result in rapid life changes. While I was going through this self-exploration, I needed to understand why I was so afraid to be my authentic self and why I didn't have the courage earlier in life to stand up for myself and to be who deep down inside I wanted to be.

My chart, below, gave me insight into why I felt this way. I have also included areas of my family chart to show how their Design has affected me throughout my life.

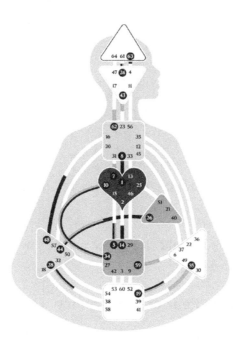

Michelle Williams's Human Design Chart

While exploring what my Human Design and conditioning meant, I found that my main theme in this life was to learn courage, self-worth, vitality, and authenticity. This was a huge eye-opener for me because I struggled with all these things throughout my life. The validation of this modality is what I needed to really find my identity. I was learning exactly what the chart told me, but I had spent my life resisting, preventing true expansion into my life purpose.

While exploring these areas more, the Spleen Center, the center for fears, spoke to me. If I was to learn courage, I needed to break through the fears which would then lead to feeling worthy and authentic with an understanding of my true vibrant self. Below is my Spleen Center.

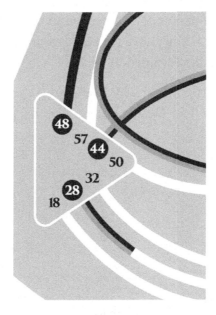

Associating each gate with the areas in my life where I have felt struggle was a good starting point.

When looking back at my life, I could clearly see patterns in my defined gates where each of these fears were very apparent.

Gate 48–Wisdom, Depth, Fear of Inadequacy

I am a habitual learner. I overcompensated this Design with earning two master's degrees and I very clearly held myself back from expanding into my soul's purpose for a long time. When intuitively tuning in, I clearly saw my soul feeling very uncomfortable and fearfully giving a piece of myself to the mission of understanding the depth and uniqueness of myself in this life and helping others do the same. I then saw several repeating past life and ancestral patterns of these lessons failing. I felt the fear deep within me as I worked through it to bring it to a resolution. As I saw and energetically released these fears and past experiences, I felt something spectacular open within me!

Gate 44–Truth, Energy, Fear of the Past

Throughout my life, I have relived situations. I'd replay conversations in my head and wish I said something different or acted differently. I always felt like I did things wrong or not the way others would, and I'd emotionally beat myself up for it. I would attract the same type of people into my life who would trigger feelings of being undeserving of love. This caused me to lose my self-worth and value. It became so normal, that I thought everyone had the same thoughts and patterns too, so it couldn't be changed—it was "normal." Through healing, I came to find out that the regrets and self-judgment that I felt were from past life and ancestral programming to teach me lessons about self-worth. The relief that I felt when I realized it was "just a lesson" was completely life changing. Through this defined gate, I have found that part of my purpose is to help others disentangle themselves from their past patterns to find true value within themselves. I have strong intuitive abilities that allow me to easily bring others to past lives and ancestral trauma to allow them to heal.

Gate 28–Adventure, Challenge, Struggle, Fear of Life Having No Meaning

As a child, I lost much of my voice and sense of value when I was taught that life had no purpose. Human Design has brought to light key information about my life purpose and helped me resolve the fears of life having no meaning. Shifting from the struggle of this gate into adventure and curiosity has opened a new meaning of life for me. It has brought on a new sense of freedom that has allowed me to heal ancestral wounds related to the fear of nothingness. I have found that these wounds are deeply integrated from my Native American heritage. I now feel valuable in the world and am excited about helping others understand their purpose and the meaning of life.

The reason I was not living to the optimal expression of the above gates made complete sense to me. The healing was well on its way, and I noticed significant changes in my life very quickly. But there was more. The open gates on my Spleen Center were also very heavily influenced by the energies around me throughout my entire life. The most interesting thing that I learned while looking through the details of these gates and relating back to my life so far, is how my conditioning was influenced by my family. Every single open gate in my Spleen was defined by my family. Not only was I absorbing all of *their* fears, but I was also amplifying them within myself! No wonder I had no idea who I was!

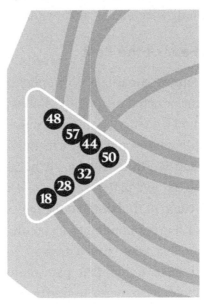

The image above is the Spleen Center that includes the definition from my family, for a comparison to my Spleen Center above. All gates are defined which means as a child, the energies and fears of these gates were apparent in my life which heavily influenced my feelings and actions.

Gate 57–Instinct, Intuition, Fear of the Future

I never quite understood why I prevented myself from visualizing and being excited about my future. I learned through schooling that the future was uncontrollable, and I brought my defined Gate 44 energy in to relive the past instead. Along with influences from schooling, I also picked up the energies from my brother's Gate 57 definition. Living in the same household with him for fifteen years caused this energy to be a part of my everyday life without even realizing it! I had a great fear of the future because I was taught that I needed to control everything around me and the future couldn't be controlled. Clearing this conditioning using energy healing techniques opened doors of creation within me. Rather than fearing the future, I now know that I am the creator of my future. My direction in life is now clear, and I have the courage to create it!

Gate 50–Nurturing, Values, Fear of Responsibility

Throughout my life, I held a deep sense of responsibility for others. I would get upset when people wouldn't listen to my advice when I could clearly see an issue about to occur. I would blame myself for the circumstances of others. I had a lot of built-up guilt for the situations that other people were in, even though it had nothing to do with me. These patterns were learned and absorbed during childhood. My entire immediate family has Gate 50 defined. This caused me to pick up these energies from three people and amplify them from each person every single day until I was eighteen years old. The sense of responsibility has been incredibly strong throughout my life and has become significantly less since I discovered that it needed to be deconditioned. I now understand that everyone is creating their life and their circumstances, and I easily let go of the need to control their situations and instead, shift into a place of love and support, if they ask.

Gate 32–Endurance, Continuity, Fear of Failure and
Gate 18–Re-alignment, Correction, Perfectionism

Similar to Gate 50, my entire family has the Gates 32 and 18 defined which significantly increased perfectionism and a fear of failure. I was fearful of disappointing people, God, and myself which caused me to adapt my life to the expectancies of others. The excruciatingly strong fear that I would fail if I did anything outside of the norm kept a deep sense of control over me. I adapted my life to what society, family, and friends wanted for me instead of following my heart. I held myself back in so many ways because things were not perfect, or I wasn't good enough to do what I wanted. The deconditioning process for these gates has been incredibly freeing. I now approach situations with curiosity and patience rather than control, allowing for creativity to flow along with a sense of playfulness and excitement for new endeavors.

As I explored my energy and my Human Design chart, I deconditioned to move out of the shadow of myself. What I found was that it was easy! My life started to shift from struggle to flow in radical ways, and very quickly. People changed toward me, and I toward them. People who no longer needed to be a part of my life left easily, and those who are here to help me grow have stayed. I am no longer a victim to my circumstances, and I have a deep understanding that change is a part of life—it's actually fun!

We are programmed to be afraid of change, to think life is hard, and to become attached to the people in our life.

The deconditioning process to bring back your light and your true, authentic self can be as simple or as difficult as you want to make it. Everyone is different and we all have different healing paths, priorities, and lessons to learn. Understanding the difference between what we are here to learn in this life and the energies that are influencing us, is life changing. It gives a sense of direction and a life mission to complete, resulting in feeling valuable and purposeful.

As I continue to work through deconditioning, I am breaking through the fears every day and finding myself, my happiness, and my life. This is the true awakening. I have been able to understand my purpose and take steps needed to shift myself easily onto that path. I have been able to take off the mask of who I was not and become my authentic self that is meant to shine a light on the world.

Listening to my inner guidance to advance me into a place of comfort was the best choice I have ever made. The validation that I could change my life without disrupting those around me was incredibly freeing. It helped me get my voice back. So much so that I moved several states away from my hometown because it felt right. There was no resistance, guilt, or fear and I am loving every minute of it! Life is in flow.

I'm here to tell you life is glorious on the other side of this fear. Deconditioning fears and other areas of your Human Design will shift you into a world of flow and magic, into true awakening. You will become the true authentic self that you are supposed to be—the optimal expression of you—which is your birth right. We are supposed to live with an abundance of happiness, prosperity, well-being, and joy—and we can!

Michelle Williams

Bestselling CoAuthor, Master Transformational
Coach, Spiritual Teacher, Certified Quantum
Human Design™ Specialist

4/1 Time Bender (Manifesting Generator)

Michelle Williams was named Top Integrative Hypnotherapist & Healing Expert for the Northern Virginia region in 2020 and has been featured on Close-up radio, MSNBC, Oprah Winfrey Network, BRAVO, and other television networks. She utilizes many professional, spiritual, and practical tools to assist her clients and students in transcending their lives through purposeful creation, inner peace, and authenticity.

Michelle's core mission is to help others reclaim their power and value through awareness, connection, and alignment with divine timing and order. By using her deep intuitive abilities and skills to identify and transform past patterns that are restricting vitality in life, she helps others experience rapid, life-altering, consistent forward movement towards truth, abundance, and their soul purpose. She believes that everyone holds the key to their own power, abundance, and optimal wellbeing.

Michelle is excited to support you through the journey to your purposeful life by providing exclusive information and offers on her website at:

IAMmichellewilliams.com/purposebydesignbook

Every step in the direction of well-being and healing leads you closer to your true self.

Michelle received several information technology degrees and an MBA while working in the corporate world before she found her divine purpose to be in service to others. She is originally from Maryland, USA and is currently living in a 100+ year old colonial home and healing space in Milledgeville, Georgia, USA with her energetic Generator yellow Labrador retriever, Sandy.

Follow Michelle on Instagram, Facebook, and YouTube @iammichellewilliams2

Acknowledgments

Collaborating with those who were brave enough to share their stories has been a joy. Thank you so much to all of these talented and gifted authors:

Alana Heim

Caroline M. Sabbah

Corissa Stepp

Elenique Marie Pizziolo

Grace Gravestock

Jes Francis

Klara Prosova

Lisa Robinett

Michelle Williams

Sharon Schneider

To Michelle Vandepas and Karen Curry Parker, cofounders of GracePoint Publishing, who guided these authors through telling their stories, we extend deep gratitude. This book would not exist without your leadership.

Deep appreciation goes to our GracePoint team, starting with Project Coordinator Carly Fahey-Dima who kept communication moving forward; continuing with the editing team of Amy Delcambre, Laurie Knight, and Debby Levering who worked with each author to ensure thoughts morphed into sentences; and completing with the design team of Clementine Kornder, Ariel Austill, and Kristina Edstrom who took extraordinary care to arrange these words and images forming the book you hold in your hands.

This Human Design compilation book is a team effort and together, through this book, we can spread the work of Human Design to people worldwide.

Books in the
Life by Human Design Series

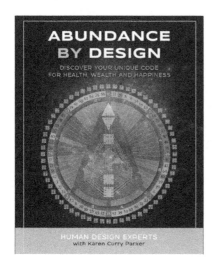

Purchase on Amazon

If you are a Human Design thought leader and want to contribute to a
future Life by Human Design book, please contact
publisher@gracepointpublishing.com.

For more great books from Human Design Press
Visit Books.GracePointPublishing.com

If you enjoyed reading *Purpose by Design* and purchased it through an online retailer, please return to the site and write a review to help others find the book.

Made in the USA
Las Vegas, NV
12 June 2024

91044794R00083